CRYSTAL BEACH
THE GOOD OLD DAYS

By ERNO ROSSI M.A.

In the Beginning

In the beginning there was heaven and earth. And on the earth there was a heavenly place called Crystal Beach.

CRYSTAL BEACH
THE GOOD OLD DAYS

By ERNO ROSSI, M.A.

BOOKS BY ERNO ROSSI

Many Cultures - Many Heritages

Nombreuses Cultures - Héritages Varie

FULL MOON

White Death - Blizzard of '77

WHITE DEATH - The Blizzard of '77 - Millennium Edition
(new revised edition)

CRYSTAL BEACH - THE GOOD OLD DAYS

Dedication

To all who enjoyed the magic of Crystal Beach.

CRYSTAL BEACH
THE GOOD OLD DAYS

By ERNO ROSSI M.A.

Seventy Seven Publishing,
147 Tennessee Avenue,
Port Colborne, Ontario
Canada L3K 2R8

Tel: 905-835-8051
Fax: 905-835-2928
Email: erossi3@cogeco.ca
Please visit me at www.whitedeath.com

Please send me your Crystal Beach stories and photos for possible inclusion in the next edition of this book.

Mail orders by check or money order to Seventy Seven Publishing, 147 Tennessee Avenue, Port Colborne, Ontario, Canada L3K 2R8.

This gift book shipped around the world and personally signed to your gift-instructions. I ship the book(s) to the address that you supply.

Mail order costs:
$24.95 plus $7.00 for postage, handling and insurance

ISBN: 0-920926-04-5

Layout & Design:
2 Suns Graphic Design - Email: darlene.teeuwsen@sympatico.ca

Printed in Canada

Acknowledgements

Thank you to all who contributed to this book.
A special thank you to the following:

Cathy Herbert — Miss Crystal Beach
Rick Herbert
Louis McDermott
Harvey Holzworth
Mary Delmont
Olaf Fub
Lon Hudkins
Sue Guenther
Jane Davies
Jude Scott
Patricia Virgil
Paul Kassay
Joan and Bill Harms
Karen and Rob Kremble
Janet Weaver
Audrey Murray
Richard Bonner
Fred Truckenbrodt
Janet Truckenbrodt
George Hutchings
Tim Rebstock
Gerry Rossi
Darlene Teeuwsen

The Buffalo News
The Fort Erie, Niagara Falls, and Port Colborne Public library
The Buffalo and Erie County Historical Society Research Library
The Buffalo State College Archives
Southtowns Walleye
Fort Erie Historical Museum
Norton Auctioneers
Coaster Enthusiasts of Canada
Niagara Farmers' Monthly
Gene Pagetto, Colonial Antique Centre, Fort Erie
Alfred F. Sagon-King, Marine Photographer
James Kay, Coaster Globe.com

Contents

In the Beginning

In the beginning there was heaven and earth. And on the earth there was a heavenly place called Crystal Beach.

"Crystal Beach started as a police village."
Ken Ellsworth

Crystal Beach started as a police village. It was very small and had three trustees in charge who were appointed every year. A summer post office opened in 1896 and a year-round post office in 1908. Incorporation of The Village of Crystal Beach into a normal village occurred in 1921 with a permanent population of 298 people. Crystal Beach was then absorbed by the City of Fort Erie in 1970 under a regional government.

" ...a boy lying prostrate, so seasick that he could not move."
Bertie Township Herald, 1921

The cruise of The Dove in 1890 was the forerunner of the present-day excursion business to Crystal Beach. Boats other than The Dove that plowed the turbulent waters between Buffalo and Crystal Beach included the Superior, Premier, State of New York, Cole, Idlewild, Timon, Pilgrim, Puritan, Gazelle, Argyle, White Star and The Pearl, afterwards renamed, The Crystal. There was another named The Ossifrage, but that was too difficult for use by people on their vacation, so she was familiarly known as the Sassy-Fras.

BAD WEATHER-NO BOATS

These boats differed from the Americana and Canadiana. They did not venture out if the weather was a bit rough. The Idlewild, for instance, had her smokestack jerked out by a heavy sea off Windmill Point. While the Timon, which was long and narrow, rolled so badly that the company kept her but one year. The story is related that the captain of the Timon walking around the deck saw a boy lying prostrate, so sea-sick that he could not move. The captain was touched with pity and said, "Young man, why don't you get a lemon and eat it. It will make you feel better." The boy feebly raised his head and said, "I did, there it is."

1

The Gazelle was worthy of her name and was a particularly frisky little boat whenever the waters of Lake Erie were a little agitated. But she was safe and easy to handle so the company kept her for some years.

One time, the management tried to turn Crystal Beach into a kind of Chautauqua and organized what was called "The International Assembly", of which Dr. Thomas Snyder was the chancellor; a Mr. George Mains was president. The Royal Hotel was built to be the Assembly Hall for this organization. The International assembly was in operation just one season, during which time the famous southern evangelist, Sam Jones, was among the speakers.

In rambling about Crystal Beach in the early days, one might have dropped into more side-shows of a circus nature than there are today. Among the attractions that stand out in memory because of real merit were the Wild West shows and the Japanese Tumblers. Then there was the Story Musical Family, perhaps better known as The Seven Singing Evangelists.

In those early days, Crystal Beach was a cheap place to live all summer. Eggs were 12 ½ cents a dozen, spring chickens 25 cents each, peas 25 cents a peck, the finest butter 18 cents a pound and milk that was full of real cream was only 5 cents for an imperial quart. Natural gas, for those who had to pay, was cheaper even than in Buffalo, while those who gave to the company the right of way across their land could burn all they wanted all year round for nothing.

The Peg Leg Railroad

Henry Beecher and Nathan Fuller built the "Peg Leg Railroad" in 1896 between Ridgeway and Crystal Beach. Ontario's first monorail ran from ten to thirty feet above ground for one and a half miles. At Ridgeway, this single-rail railroad connected to the Grand Trunk Railway that carried people to larger urban centers such as Buffalo, New York.

"... a squall caught the Pearl as she was pulling out from the Crystal Beach dock."

George J. Rebstock

Possibly the most dramatic thing that happened was the night a squall caught the Pearl as she was pulling out from the Crystal Beach dock with about 1000 passengers on board and swung it around at right angles to the dock and rested her on the bottom. The Puritan which had just left with her load of passengers for Buffalo, noticing the plight of her sister ship, came back and tried to pull the Pearl off, but was unsuccessful.

The crew of the Pearl managed to get a plank runway from the boat to the dock and a human chain passed passengers to safety. Later the Puritan made a return trip from Buffalo and everyone got back to Buffalo with no casualties. Two or three times in the early days, storms wrecked the dock, which had to be almost entirely rebuilt.

"...but the bout was of short duration."

George J. Rebstock

One of the ministers we had in those days, the Rev. J.H. McBain, was quite a well-built husky man who was interested in getting people out to church. The Reverend met with Ol. Nicks at his blacksmith shop. The minister went there on a wintry morning with his horse to be shod. The place was full of young fellows as it was too stormy to go fishing. They had the boxing gloves on. The Parson introduced himself and said that he would like to have his horse shod. Nicks replied, "Well yes, but let's have a bout first." The Parson's reply was, "Oh no, it would not be the thing for me to do, people might talk about it..."

After some words that hinted that the Parson might be a little bit yellow, the Parson agreed to put on the gloves. But the bout was of short duration. Mr. Nicks had to be pulled out of the corner of the shop as one blow from the Parson's strong arm had knocked-out Mr. Nicks. He got up rather meekly and shod the horse and afterwards became a steady church-goer and one of Mr. McBain's stalwart supporters.

"We called him Hon Kong."

George J. Rebstock

During the first few years we were here, we had an interesting character in these parts. We called him Hon Kong. He lived in a cave north west of Sheehab's Hotel and went around the countryside picking up food. As the cottages began to grow up, he didn't like it so he disappeared.

The Assembly House

The Assembly House on the beach was the largest of the hotels at that time. It housed regular guests and entertainers. Later named The Royal, it was destroyed by fire in 1923.

"... lose that $20 gold piece."

George J. Rebstock

The proprietor of the Assembly House was a Dr. Thomas Snyder, a medical doctor and lay preacher. He always liked to tell the story of the man who put the $20 gold piece on the collection plate by mistake. After the service, he went up to the Doctor and explained how it happened, how he had a silver dollar in one pocket and the gold piece in another. The Doctor was pretty shrewd and didn't want to lose that $20, so after some quick thinking, he said, "Well sir, if you can prove it was not God's plan that you were to put that gold piece on the collection plate you can have it back." He didn't get it back.

"... 12 to 15 boats leaving the foot of Buffalo's Main Street."

George J. Rebstock

At the turn of the century, there were 12 to 15 boats leaving the foot of Buffalo's Main Street for different resorts along the lake and Niagara River, besides the Detroit-Buffalo and the Buffalo-Cleveland boats. Today, there is only the one; and the day may come when it will not be profitable to operate that. I hope it is a long way off.

Crystal Beach dock, boats and visitors in 1894.
Cathy Herbert Collection

"After the first war started in 1914 we heard a strange noise and we ran outside and saw our first airplane."

Howard Fretz

I was born in 1904 in Ridgeway on the Gilmore road. My Number 14 school was built in 1911 and was a mile away by road but half a mile when I walked across the fields. In the summer we went barefoot.

If the weather was bad my father or a neighbor would give us a ride to school in a horse drawn buggy and then pick us up after school. My school had about 20 students and the grades were the premier to grade eight. We used to call them junior premier, senior premier, junior first, senior first, junior second and senior second. That's the way it went up to senior fourth.

Our one room school was heated by natural gas but when that didn't work we burned wood. We had a basement that had water in it and the water would freeze in winter. Then we were allowed to go skating in the basement in the winter.

On certain days we would not have recess so that we could have a longer lunch hour. Then we could go across the fields to the woods where there was a nice pond where we skated. I had an old pair of wooden skates with a file for blades that curved up at the toes. We strapped on the skates to our boots and they were really good skates.

I never had a store-bought hockey stick when I went to school. We'd get a nice curved stick out of the woods and we had a great time playing hockey.

On Arbor Day we had to clean up around the school. I enjoyed that. We had to cut the lawn with a little push mower. We would hook each other up and one person would pull and two or three others would push.

One day on the way home from school we saw a lot of smoke across the fields. My grandfather was thrashing with a steam engine and the sparks lit the barn on fire and the barn burned down.

Another time, after the First World War started in 1914, we heard a strange noise. We ran outside and there was an airplane flying overhead, just a small airplane and it was the first plane that we had ever seen.

Soon after we heard another strange noise and we saw a bunch of soldiers who marched from Port Colborne to Fort Erie. We ran outside and watched them march past.

Our Christmas concert was really special. We had drills, plays, songs, and candy--the works. Those were wonderful times.

When our church had baptisms we'd go out on Point Abino Road and hold the baptisms in Lake Erie.

Clarence Teal ice delivery.
Cathy Herbert Collection

In winter when we traveled by open buggy we would put three live rabbits in a bag and place them over our feet. Then a blanket covered the rabbits and our feet. Other times we would warm up stove lids and stones and put them under a cover by our feet. We even put a coal oil lantern under the rug and that kept us warm. There were no lights on our buggies or wagons but there was never an accident. In the winter we would hear the sleighs being pulled on Point Abino Road or the Burger Road. Every neighbor had a different sounding bell and we could identify the neighbors by the sound of their sleigh bells.

We crossed over to Buffalo on the ferry at Fort Erie. My Dad would take samples of his marrow beans and take orders in Buffalo at the Chippewa Market and the A&P store. After the Peace Bridge was completed in 1927 we would take a team of horses across the bridge and deliver beans in downtown Buffalo with the horses.

In the summer there were the Americana and the Canadiana that made trips to Crystal Beach from Buffalo. You could leave and return on the hour on these boats. There was also a little launch for the people of Point Abino. Many Americans lived there and they could come by launch or by train. There was a train station at Point Abino. Here there were buses that consisted of big wagons with seats along the sides and horses drew them. Local people made a business of transporting homeowners and visitors to their destinations.

West of Crystal Beach is Bay Beach and I worked for a man there for three years in carpentry and painting during the spring and fall. This man owned

Round and round on the Razzle Dazzle.
Harvey Holzworth Collection

two icehouses. In the winter we took a horse with an ice-plow out onto the frozen surface of Lake Erie. The horse would plough the square ice junks about two feet square and about eight inches to a foot thick. The local farmers would come around with their teams of horses. A gang of men would be on the lake cutting the ice junks and filling their sleighs. Another gang would be at the icehouse where they packed the ice blocks closely together. Around the sides of the ice was packed about eight inches of sawdust. The ice was well preserved until summer. Then we took the old horse and wagon and delivered the ice to customers along the lakeshore.

I knew the name of every American from Point Abino Road to the entrance of Crystal Beach. Then one day my boss Joe Adams said to me that I didn't need to deliver ice into this one house because Mr. Benner had an electric icebox. You could hear the thing running all the way out to Erie Road. That's the first time that I heard of a refrigerator.

"Hotdogs were expensive at Crystal Beach."

My name is Edward Homer Hawkins and I was born in 1916 in Stevensville. When we were kids, the Farmers' Picnic at Crystal Beach was a really big thing for Fort Erie, Stevensville and the surrounding district. Hotdogs were more expensive at Crystal Beach. Hotdogs and soda pop cost ten cents each. Other places you paid five cents each.

Fletcher Teal

The road east of Derby Road is Ridge Road and the rides at the park used to come out to Ridge Road. There was a big band shell there as well and singers came there and sang their songs. The old ballroom was plain compared to the new ballroom that came much later. They used whitewash on the outside of the old ballroom so that you came away white if you brushed up against it.

Parachute Jumper-1919

On July 5, 1919, Frank Ellis was the first person in Canada to parachute from a plane at Crystal Beach.

The plane that dropped the parachutist, 1919.
Cathy Herbert Collection

"...it was like floating on air when you were dancing."

Ross Valvo

Those were horse and buggy days when my dad bought his first car. We had a barn in the back of the house that we used as a garage. My dad drove his car inside the barn and crashed through the back of the barn and out into the open barnyard. That was the end of his driving days.

Crystal Beach was a beautiful place. I liked to dance and they had a big dance hall there. I was courting my wife then and we used to go up there dancing. I worked there for one summer at a restaurant so I knew the guy who took the tickets. I bought only one ticket for five cents and the guy wouldn't take it off me so that ticket lasted me all night. It was a beautiful dance floor. It was like floating on air when you were dancing.

Juniati family cottage.
Harvey Holzworth Collection

We loved the Canadiana. We'd drive to Buffalo, park our car, board the Canadiana, dance on the boat on the way to Crystal Beach, dance in the Crystal Ballroom, dance on the last boat back to Buffalo and then drive home.

"I used to work as a dishwasher at the Erie Beach Train Station."

My Dad had a barbershop in Fort Erie called Butler's Barbershop on Courtwright St. The Dummy that used to go back and forth to Black Rock used to dock at Courtwright St. and discharge passengers. The Dummy was very reasonable and was used by people at the north end of Fort Erie to cross the Niagara River. Otherwise, you had to go to the south end of Fort Erie and use the more expensive ferryboat to cross the river to Buffalo. This was all before the Peace Bridge was built in 1927.

At the ferry landing I used to catch a train to Erie Beach where I worked as a dishwasher at the Erie Beach Train Station. In time, the depression of the 1930's and the Crystal Beach Amusement Park put the Erie Beach Amusement Park out of business.

Cyclone 1939.
Photo by and courtesy of Alfred Sagon-King

Lost Legends: Crystal Beach Cyclone

By James Kay, Coaster Globe.com

The 1920's was the golden age of roller coasters. It is estimated that over 1500 were standing in the "roaring twenties." This was an age of innovation and experimentation, an age of Traver, Prior and Church. Many of the greatest coasters of all time were constructed in this decade: Riverview Bobs, Rye Airplane…to name a few. But one coaster shines above all the others in the minds of roller coaster enthusiasts: The Cyclone at Crystal Beach, Ontario, Canada.

In 1927, the Crystal Beach Park added two new rides, both of them designed by one of the legendary figures of the amusement park industry: Harry Guy Traver. One of the new rides was one of Traver's incredibly popular "Tumble Bug" rides. The other was the Cyclone roller coaster. The Cyclone was one of the so-called "Traver Trio," the three identical coasters built in 1927. The other two were the Lightning at Revere Beach and the Cyclone at Palisades Park. These three nearly identical coasters are among the most thrilling coasters of all time. Unfortunately, the Lightning and the Palisades Cyclone lasted six and seven years respectively. The Cyclone at Crystal Beach, however, survived the depression of the 1930's and lived a relatively long and prosperous life.

On its opening day in 1927, the Cyclone drew an estimated 75000 people to Crystal Beach. The crowds broke down fences and gates just to get a good view of its twisted drops and curves. Several riders were so impressed with the Cyclone that they rode it more than fifty times on its first few days of operation. The ride was so intense that there was a full time nurse on duty at all times to revive riders who had passed out.

The Cyclone began with what has been called the best drop ever. A steep drop-off made to appear to riders that the cars were going straight into Lake Erie. Then, it twisted sharply to the right in a great swooping curve. Next, it plunged into a straight drop alongside its lift hill. After that the Cyclone dove into a spiralling helix angled at 70 degrees. Then, without letting up for an instant, riders were dropped into a high-speed figure-eight section. Next, after a dive inside the first drop, the trains entered a series of abrupt drops. Next came the famous trick-track, where the track banked rapidly from side to side. Finally, after a couple more turns, came the brake run. The total trip from top of the first drop to the station brakes was only forty seconds.

In September of 2000, we had a chance to interview Ed. Mills. Ed rode the Cyclone in 1945, one year before it closed. This is what he remembers of

Crystal Beach and the Cyclone:

"Then I screamed two words during the Cyclone roller coaster ride, "JESUS CHRIST!" Ed Mills.

My most memorable ride in an amusement park occurred in July 1945, when I was on military leave in St. Catharines, Ontario, Canada. I had just turned 18 and had been in the Canadian Army for about 8 months. My two buddies and I spent a part of our leave in Crystal Beach, Ontario. It was the greatest place for servicemen to have a good time.

Besides, Crystal Beach was famous for having the most thrilling roller coaster ride in the Western Hemisphere. We were well-trained soldiers for any kind of warfare and we feared nothing — except the Military Police. And since we were on a legal pass, there was nothing to fear.

We aimed for the roller coaster with the huge sign that said, The Cyclone — Thrill of a Lifetime. Loud screams came from the coaster as we bought our tickets for 15 or 20 cents. We then stood in the line-up near the entrance gate that happened to be very close to where the previous passengers got off. It was then that I noticed the distinctive smell of vomit, which was stronger as we got closer to the loading point.

It was a bit disconcerting, but I was then hit in the face. A wallet had fallen from the ride. We opened it and it had a U.S. Navy ID Card in it. As soon as the ride stopped, we saw the American sailor get off the ride and I called to him. He looked a bit dazed. And he didn't know the fate of his wallet until I gave it to him.

Then it was our turn to ride and we jumped into the coaster cars. Up the steep ramp we went, up, up and then some more until we could see the entire amusement park. Just as I was enjoying the view, the car lurched forward and I looked in front of me down a steep incline that looked to be an 89-degree slope. The cars then roared down the incline at warp speed and all I could see in front of us was Lake Erie. I was sure that there must have been a part of the tracks missing. Then I screamed only two words during the entire ride…"JESUS CHRIST"… as we plunged down towards the lake. I then saw a steep bank to the right of the incline and we changed directions in a split second, turning on our side as the car careened around a hairpin turn. I looked sideways and saw the earth spinning by and from that point onward, most of the ride was pretty much of a blur.

Another memorable part occurred when we reached a high horizontal. We were racing around a curve at such speed that it seemed certain that we would fly off into thin air. Frankly I was quite relieved to see the cars finally slow down. Even then, they approached the unloading platform at such a speed that I thought that we would overshoot and crash into the spectators.

When I walked off the unloading platform, I smelled the vomit again and I walked away from the area in order to resettle my stomach.

———

On September 2, 1946, the Cyclone closed forever. Its wicked intensity was too great for a public that was no longer as thrill-seeking as they were in the twenties. On September 16, the dismantling of the Cyclone began. Some of the wood and steel from the Cyclone was used by John Allen and Herbert Schmeck (both designers for the Philadelphia Toboggan Company) in the construction of PTC Coaster #112, the Crystal Beach Comet in 1948.

When Crystal Beach closed in 1989, the Comet was sold at auction. It reopened in 1994 at the Great Escape (Lake George, New York) where it still operates today.

The Cyclone is considered by many roller coaster enthusiasts today to be the most thrilling coaster ever built. Its relentless pacing and intensity has never been matched. Its first drop has been copied, but has never been done as well as the original. Its status as a Lost Legend is truly unquestionable.

Statistics

Height:	29.3m (96′)
Length:	900m (2953′)
Max Speed:	96kph (60mph)
Ride Time	1:10
Inversions:	0
Year:	1927-1946
Designer:	Harry G. Traver
Type:	Wood
Layout:	Twister
Restraints:	Lap Bar
Power:	Chain Lift
Max Vertical Gs:	4
Cost:	$176,000

"I remember a ride that was located in the water, right near the dock and it would twirl around."

Harvey Holzworth

I was born in 1924 and we lived in Buffalo. My dad bought a summer home, cottage #71, on the top of the hill, on the waterfront at Crystal Beach. As a baby, I could listen to the band music coming off the Crystal Beach Boat. We loved those sounds along with the merriment of people down on the beach. Those were the days when there was no fence on the beach. There was also a sidewalk down on the beach in front of the homes. Parts of it are still visible when the sand washes away. Honey Teal used to deliver ice to us.

At that time, the Canadiana and the Americana were the two boats that arrived at the dock. The Crystal Ballroom had a bandstand in the middle of the dance floor.

I also remember the Royal Ballroom at the old Royal Hotel, located at the Bay Beach end of Crystal Beach. Mr. Rebstock owned it and used it for summer apartments.

I can remember a ride that was located in the shallow water, right near the dock. That ride would twirl around and the swimmers would grab hold of it and swing sideways out into the air and then let go and splash into the water.

Sea Swing.
Harvey Holzworth Collection

The Ferris Wheel.
Harvey Holzworth Collection

15

Canadiana underway to Crystal Beach in 1946.
Courtesy of Buffalo State College, Courier Collection

Thrills, Chills and Cinnamon Suckers

By George Kunz—Courtesy, Buffalo News

Crystal Beach Day was summer's high point and like all great occasions, it had to be provided for. My brother and I would scour the neighborhood collecting Buffalo Evening News coupons for reduced-rate tickets; these we would husband like misers. We made lists of the amusements and rides; we decided which one to go on first, which we would ride most frequently. We studied weather forecasts because nothing could be worse than rain on Crystal Beach Day.

Those were hard times—the Depression of the 1930's—and there were limits on what families could spend for recreation. But we were among the lucky ones, in this respect at least. For us there was still that special day—the trip across the water, the picnic and especially the loops and twists and giddy downhill plunges of the rides.

Each year, as the day grew nearer, our happy memories from past Crystal Beach Days grew sharper and our impatience for the new one increased.

As I recall, the first boat left from the foot of Commercial Street at 10 a.m. My mother would have packed a lunch the night before and this we carried in a basket to the South Park streetcar stop. Then came the first of the endless waits: a wait for the streetcar to begin and another for the streetcar ride to end. After we climbed down the trolley steps, there was the walk with many other expectant children and their parents down Commercial Street and through the tunnel to the Crystal Beach Transit Office. As we emerged from the tunnel, we saw the Crystal Beach boat waiting. Noble and gleaming in the morning sunshine, the Canadiana seemed to me to represent the ultimate in luxury and pleasure.

After waiting in a long line, we bought our tickets. Then began the next wait. Inside a large, damp enclosure we sat waiting, like immigrants, for a cyclone fence door to be opened. With maddening leisure, the crewmen laid the gangways and examined the boat before finally opening the gates. Then out lunged screaming children with parents in tow, across the planks and onto the boat.

Once aboard, we began our annual boat-ride ritual. We walked along the first deck to the engine room. Ever immaculate, hot and smelling of lubricant, the boilers were a masterwork of efficiency. Huge pistons began to move, and we could hear the swish of moving water as the boat pulled away from Buffalo.

My mother, with our lunch basket, by this time would be stationed sedately in a cane-seated chair on the second deck. This was our base; here we would meet if we lost one another.

Meanwhile we wildly explored the boat. We chased one another up flights fore and aft and ran along the extended third deck and down the stairway to an enclosed, wood-paneled second-deck room where the old people gathered. Here a certain decorum prevailed, and we slowed our pace accordingly. Behind this room, music played and a few couples danced.

The boat ride lasted about 45 minutes and that was enough. We had our fill of darting around the boat by then. And anyway, once Crystal Beach came into view, everything else lost its luster. We could see the sprawling amusement park and hear the sounds of rides coming to life. The huge Ferris wheel was turning; there were high-pitched whistles and toots from the little train, clanks and roars of wheels from the roller coasters.

Then came more endless waits, now all the more encompassing. There was the tedium of the boat's docking. We watched heavy ropes secured about stanchions and the gangways thrown down. And then there was the rush up the long concrete pier covered with corrugated metal, to the entrance turnstiles.

I could never understand the complications of customs. They were an annoyance at best, and we could barely contain ourselves within view of the old familiar rides that we had been dreaming of since we left them last year.

But to be detained only to be asked some idiot questions like, "Where were you born?" — What a bit of adult foolishness!

Finally we were through the turnstile and in the park. To the left lay the beach. We could look through the chicken-wire fence separating it from the park and see people swimming or sitting on the beach, reading and soaking up the sun. It looked inviting, but our interests were elsewhere.

It was about noon, and though we were practically jumping with expectation, my Mother made us have lunch. So into the grove behind the restaurant we went.

By this time the amusements were in full operation. There were the roars of wheels, the ecstatic screams of passengers and the merry-go round music. The familiar aroma of waffles, hamburgers and onions drifted by.

Poor Mother realized the extent of her popularity, and in her defense, she tried to make lunch as quick and painless as possible. When we had finished our sandwiches, we were shouting for tickets for the rides, anxious to be off.

I can remember Mother encouraging us to begin with the merry-go-round or the little train. I was puzzled at the time because I wanted to begin with the roller coaster, but I know now that Mother had a sense of climax — and good common sense as well. "Let them ride the gentler rides first or they never will," she must have thought. I understood her strategy years later when I took my own children to Crystal Beach.

So the merry-go-round, always orderly, well kept and freshly painted, was first. Mother rode with us. She sat on one of the benches, while each of us mounted a wolf, a lion or a Llama, or one of the animals in the two inner circles where the carved figures bounded up and down.

After that we went on the little train, pulled by a locomotive that actually was a miniature steam engine, fueled with coal. I can recall getting hot cinders in my eyes, in spite of the grids behind the engine and in front of many cars that were supposed to trap the flying specks. Smiling approvingly, Mother rode the little train with us.

We then graduated to more dynamic devices. There was the "Hey-Day," where if you rode the back seat you were swung around on the steel floor at a speed that made your stomach tingle. Its cars were brightly painted with the names of autos printed on their backs: Ford, Buick and Plymouth.

The "Caterpillar," a rather strange-looking invention that ran on a circular, wave-like track, was nearby. The cars simply followed the track, but at one point a striped canvas umbrella fanned out over the cars. The ride earned its name because it vaguely resembled a caterpillar.

The creators of some of these rides must have been entomologists because next came the "Tumblebug," which was very much like the

"Caterpillar." It too ran on a circular track but the waves were much higher and the tickling sensations more delightful. The Tumblebug had about six units in its train, and they did look like ladybugs. Each unit had a name, such as "June Bug" or "Lightning Bug".

We always rode the little autos too. The original ride operated electrically on the same principle as the subway. Moving between wooden guardrails, each car had an arm that touched an electrical cable on the side. The steering wheel really controlled the vehicle, and the autos resembled 1930 Chevrolets.

Cathy Herbert at Comet ruins, 1990.
Cathy Herbert Collection

When we were thirsty we had lemonade, which Mother had brought from home. Although the big glass jars of green, red and yellow beverages along the midway were enticing, we know better than to hope, let alone ask, for such luxuries in those hard times.

As a change of pace we would try the Old Mill, which later became Jungle Land. Heavy flat-bottomed boats led through endless, airless tunnels. Every so often there was a dioramic scene with a tired, obviously papier-mâché animal or specter making a jerky, menacing movement toward the boat.

One year Mother dropped her purse into the water, creating a crisis. She later would tell the story of how kind the operator had been, taking a net and straining through the water until he raised the lost purse, soaked but containing all its valuables.

Sometimes we boys would look into the dance hall with the large crystal ball suspended from the ceiling. Occasionally couples would be dancing to music from a jukebox, and we would mimic them in their dreamy display of affection.

I never liked the "Fun House," but my cousin Bill who sometimes went with us, did. The ever-turning barrel, which we had to creep through along

19

the course, made me vaguely nauseous, and I never enjoyed the little pranks: the wind machine, the electrical shocks, and the trap doors. I could appreciate that it was relatively inexpensive, although, lasting some ten minutes and taking only two tickets.

Mother had once gotten sick on the Ferris wheel and never forgot it. She always found an excuse to prevent us from riding it. I didn't mind because the big wheel seemed so awesome.

My favorite ride was the "Junior Coaster" now called the "Giant Coaster." I still consider this an excellent roller coaster. It had a frightening first hill and some good turns and dips at high speed. It was a badge of bravery to have ridden the Junior Coaster.

The "Dodg'em" was also fun. Located near the coaster, it differed very little from its descendent, the "Auto Scooters," but its cars were old and drab, and the environs always smelled of arcing electricity.

The ride that ruled over all in the noise, size and reputation was the huge roller coaster, the "Cyclone." It was unthinkable that we, mere children that we were, could ride it, but we could watch it and listen and cower before its might. The Cyclone stood beside the dance hall and always seemed to me a triumph of engineering. Compressed into a relatively small area, it appeared as a dark monster, brooding, glowering and scolding over everything. Only people older, braver, perhaps more foolish, I thought—rode it. Later in my career, I became an avid Cyclone rider.

When evening came we had another lunch, this one more welcome than the first. In the same grove as before, we could see the gypsies setting up tents on the periphery of the park, lighting candles, and putting up their signs. I was uneasy as I watched the strangely dressed people talking among themselves in odd tongues. Like their tents, an air of mystery settled over them. Lights were starting to go on all over the park. The Canadiana could be seen out on the lake as it slowly approached for its final trip back to Buffalo. The day was drawing to a tired close. Sometimes there would be a few unused tickets, which we would spend in prodigal fashion with one last ride on the roller coaster or Tumblebug.

One final ceremony remained: the buying of waffles and cinnamon suckers. Waffles were eaten either on the midway or on the boat ride home. But the cinnamon suckers were always taken home with us and consumed as the last wistful souvenirs of a great day.

By now we were much different from the children who arrived ten hours earlier. Weary, subdued and a little sad, we boarded the Canadiana, taking seats quietly beside my mother on the Middle deck. As the boat brought me back to the real world, I watched the wonders of my boyhood fade from view.

A generation later, in the mid-1960's, I returned to Crystal Beach with my own children. Gleefully, I made my toddlers walk the midway with me. "Here," I lectured, "here children stood the Cyclone." And the children had to trace the Cyclone's foundation with their mad father.

"And Jungle Land is really the Old Mill. And this was not meant to be a roller rink, but a dance hall."

At that time the little autos still operated, although they had been moved to a new site. As of old, the HEYDAY and the Caterpillar plied their courses. I had long since overcome my Mother's prejudice against the Ferris wheel and now greatly enjoyed riding it with my children.

The little train was new, diesel-powered and acceptable even though I missed the hot cinders. The Fun House had become the Magic Carpet, but what's in a name? As always, a dispassionate man sat unobtrusively masterminding the electric shocks and the jet stream of air.

The Canadiana had, of course ceased to run. But we walked out on the pier; and I pointed out the mooring posts where the boat used to dock. I also boasted that I could remember riding on its twin ship, the Americana.

In the days since the flat admission fee and the sound of rock music have overtaken the park, I haven't been back often to Crystal Beach.

But I did return once again to collect my children now of high school age. I arrived about an hour too early and a kindly guard invited me inside the park to find them.

To my sorrow, I discovered that many of my favorite rides have been displaced: the Caterpillar, the HEYDEY, both of which I thought in charity too old to be moved — the Old Mill, alias Jungle Land, the Ferris wheel and the old cars, although I spotted a few hulks used as ornaments in a field. And in addition — is nothing sacred? The dance hall now contains something called the "Jolly Roger" that creeps over the respected floors. The foundations of the old Cyclone are long since pasted over with cement or asphalt.

Two things have not changed. The cinnamon suckers, from the Hall's sucker stand, are the same as ever with their old friendly sting. On the way home my generous children produced from a battered bag some Crystal Beach waffles, which they had bought for my wife and me. Whoever concocted that recipe must have sold exclusive world rights to the Crystal Beach waffle makers. The taste is unmistakable; it is subtle and distinctive.

Many things change as time goes on; many gentle customs are replaced by harsher sights and sounds. But not childhood, not fun, not the love of parents for their children — and not Crystal Beach waffles and cinnamon suckers.

"I documented the demise of the amusement park."

Cathy Herbert

Growing up in the village of Crystal Beach was the basis for my association with the Crystal Beach Amusement Park. I am thankful that my parents came to live in Crystal Beach in 1941 and still live in the same house they moved into in 1945, where my two brothers and I grew up. My mother kept newspaper articles from the Buffalo Courier Express dating back to 1952, two years before I was born. In one sense, she began my collection of historical articles. Perhaps she knew she would have a daughter who would be interested in the history of the area. The Village of Crystal Beach and the amusement park influenced my life in many different ways.

Most of the school kids had summer jobs in the Park. I was not allowed to work there, in part due to the bad experiences that my two older brothers had. However, I think it would have been fun to have a summer job there.

The Park was a favorite hangout for local kids, although most of the young people who went to the Park were from Buffalo. Because I lived at the Beach, the Park did not hold as much fascination for me as it did for kids from Buffalo.

Each year, at the end of the school term, all school children could obtain free passes for the bathing beach. To get there, we had to walk past the Miniature Train ride. On hot days the tarmac in front of the entrance to the ride became so soft that our toes would sink into it. My brothers remember this too.

I always enjoyed the rides that I had on the various amusements. Bert Deere, who lived on our street, worked on the Old Mill, a boat ride through covered tunnels. If I was lucky enough when I walked by and said "hi" to him, he would wave me in for a free ride. This was always a thrill. Other rides I remember are The Looper, HEYDEY, Roll-O-Plane, Giant Coaster, Turnpike, Scrambler, Paratrooper, Wild Mouse, Tumble Bug, and Caterpillar to name a few. The sand hill where the flower gardens were located was another favorite spot to me.

One of the most vivid memories was the odor that came out of the washrooms in the basement of the Ballroom. These toilets were not like flush toilets at home. Rows of toilets sat above a trough of fast-flowing water. As a small child, I thought that if I fell threw the hole, I would be washed out into the lake. Because of these memories, I took advantage of the opportunity to obtain two of the toilets (and a bathroom door) when the Park was being dismantled. These toilets are probably the only ones still in existence.

I always had a love of local history, especially for Crystal Beach. From each year of my childhood, I kept Park tickets in a small cedar box, as well as postcards. Around 1980, I took a serious interest in the history of the area, which included Greater Fort Erie.

The Village of Crystal Beach was encompassed by Fort Erie in 1970 under a regional government. But the soft spot in my heart was always for my hometown, Crystal Beach.

My interest in collecting postcards lead me to postcard shows and I traveled far and wide where I discovered new cards. One thing lead to another, and I found myself wanting to collect anything related to the area. I have a special interest in souvenir china, which is not easy to find, but I have been lucky over the years to have acquired many unique pieces.

In 1984, I published a series of postcards of Greater Fort Erie, which included several from the Amusement Park. This started a small business producing items pertaining to the area. I published four calendars with old pictures of the Park, with short informative write-ups beneath each picture, for the years 1999 through 2002. My website has many pictures of the Park, as well as other items, including note cards, videos, DVD's, magnets and t-shirts, at www.crystalbeachmemories.com.

Over a two year period, 1989-1990, I documented the demise of the Amusement Park, taking a total of approximately 10,000 still photos and shooting daily video footage. In order to take these pictures, I had to climb to the top of everything, from the Comet and Giant coasters, to the roof of the Ballroom, to the top of the Arcade sign, to the top of the Carousel building. Looking back, I must have been "crazy" as I have a fear of heights.

However, what I did can't be done again.

The demolition of the world-famous Ballroom was a sad time for anyone who had experienced the excitement of the Big Band era. My dad and I were there to document the event. Paul Kassay was there too and insisted that my dad and I have one last dance on that famous floor. It was hard to dance without music, but we improvised, and Paul caught us on tape. This footage became part of the documentary video that I helped Paul to produce, along with Janet Truckenbrodt. It is called "The Life and Times of Crystal Beach", and we have sold about 8,000 copies since it went on sale in 1994, and is still selling. Many of the pictures I had in my collection were used in the making of this video as well as some VHS footage that I took after the Park closed.

An era ended in 1989 with the closing of the Park and the subsequent auction on October 17. The day before had been a beautiful and warm fall day, but the day of the auction was wet and cold, which seemed fitting for the "death" of such a famous and popular attraction. I bought some plastic chairs, and one wooden one, and that was all. The prices were in American funds, and everything seemed inflated in its value. I really wanted one of the waffle irons, as did my brother, but the price they realized was too much for us. Both my brother and I did come to own one many years after the auction.

Although I didn't buy much at the sale I was able to buy things over the years. The buyer of the Laff-in- the-Dark building sold me a car right after the Park auction and that was a great buy. I was able to purchase a car from the Giant coaster as well and have been lucky in acquiring other items from the Park.

I continue to collect, but have to pick and choose, since storage space in my house and garage is becoming limited. The thrill of finding something new for my collection never fades.

The Memory Lingers On

By Cathy Herbert

Crystal Beach Park was a world-famous attraction for more than a century. The Cyclone, the Crystal Ballroom, the Comet and especially the beach, were just a few of the elements that made this park a unique landmark.

John Evangelist Rebstock bought lakefront farm property on Lake Erie in 1888, with the intention of selling the sand to construction companies in nearby Buffalo. The company he formed was fittingly named the Lake Erie Sand Company. Fortunately, he had second thoughts about destroying such a beautiful setting.

Instead he created a religious assembly ground, "for the spiritual and mental uplift of the common people". The name "Crystal Beach" was decided upon because of the crystal-like quality of the sand and the clear sparkling water of the lake. The resort was to be a combination camp meeting ground, religious colony and Chautauqua assembly, with this central theme relieved 'by a few choice sideshow attractions".[1] When almost 150,000 people visited the area during a single season, the original idea was abandoned after two years. The sideshows that fringed the colony attracted more attention than the main program.[2]

John E. Rebstock and three associates - Arthur Hickman and William Palmer, both Buffalo attorneys, and Oliver Jenkins, a Buffalo postmaster - incorporated the Crystal Beach Company at this time.[3]

Ship to Shore

The first dock was built of log piers which were put in place during the winter through the ice and filled with stone. That dock allowed ferry service between Crystal Beach and Buffalo with the maiden voyage of the side-wheeler *Dove* on July 16, 1890. The *Pearl* followed the next year, and a long line of passenger steamers followed over the years, including the *Gazelle, Puritan, Darius Cole, Ossifrage, Argyle, Garden City, State of New York, Superior, Crystal* and *Idlewild*, some of which operated simultaneously.[4]

The Crystal Beach Steamboat and Ferry Company was organized in 1892,[5] with stocks selling at $50 each, helping to finance the excursion boats.[6] J.E. Rebstock acted as general manager, excursion agent, dock master, ticket taker and even pilot of the boat at times.[7] Though optimistic about the future of the park, Rebstock's company was slow to improve the grounds for several years because of poor attendance and weak financial support.[8]

In 1908, partly because of J.E. Rebstock's health, the Crystal Beach Company was sold to businessmen from Detroit and Cleveland, who renamed it the Lake Erie Excursion Company. This new company not only vastly changed the park's appearance by rearranging the entire layout, installing a water system, draining the land and laying out the Midway, but greatly improved the water route service between it and Buffalo. The man who engineered the changes was George Ricker; president of the company was Thomas Newman.[9]

That same year, on February 22, 1908, a new all-steel steamer was launched from the Buffalo Dry Dock Company called the *Americana*.[10] A round-trip fare to Crystal Beach cost 25 cents.

Two years later, in March 1910, an identical sister ship, the *Canadiana* was brought into service, with the exception that she was five tons heavier than the *Americana's* 969 gross tonnage.[11] Length was 214 feet, with a width of 54 feet amidships, powered by a triple-expansion steam engine developing 1,446 horsepower. The *Canadiana* had the largest dance floor of any passenger steamer on the Great Lakes, with an original capacity for 3,500 passengers.[12] The Lake Erie Excursion Company boasted of having "the two finest excursion steamers between Buffalo and Duluth Minnesota, representing a total expenditure of $500,000.[13]

The *Americana* and *Canadiana* were well served by a new Crystal Beach dock built in 1910,[14] the same year the *Canadiana* was put into service. Both boats were very busy with the park's patrons and also with the many commuters who worked in Buffalo during the day and spent their evenings and weekends at their cottages along Lake Erie.[15]

Boat passengers leaving the dock had to climb a natural sand dune in order to gain entrance to the park. A "cut" was made through this sand-hill

**Canadiana leaves Buffalo on her maiden voyage
for Crystal Beach, May 30, 1910.**

Courtesy Heritage Press

and a 200-foot concrete walkway was laid from the "cut" to the lake, replacing the old plank walkway.[16]

Popular amusement concessions at this time included the Scenic Railway roller coaster, Figure Eight, Old Mill, Miniature Railway, Aerial Swing, Merry-Go-Round, Bowling Alley and Skating Rink. Plus the old dance pavilion was enlarged and improved, including a new floor.[17]

One other major improvement to the park was the building of the third pier that opened on May 26, 1921.[18] It is still in existence today, but years of neglect have taken their toll.

Property Sold

The Lake Erie Excursion Company operated the park until it was sold to the Buffalo and Crystal Beach Corporation in March 1924, for an estimated price of one million dollars. The purchase covered all property owned by the Excursion Company, including the boats, docks in both Buffalo and Canada, the land and midway entertainment. Negotiations took three months, with the final papers being signed by George Hall Sr., president of the new corporation, which was formed by Buffalonians and Canadians.[19]

George Hall began his association with the park as a concessionaire in the early 1900's with Hall's suckers, and through the years his business grew to include popcorn, peanuts, crispettes (caramel corn), and cream chewing candy, the forerunner of the famous Hall candy kisses.[20]

More than $100,000 was spent on improvements alone in the first year of Hall's ownership, beginning with the building of the breakwall, or 'sea

Crystal Beach Stock 1924. Four shares for Buffalo and Crystal Beach Corporation valued at $100 each.

Harvey Holzworth Collection

wall".[21] Work began as soon as the ice was out of the lake in the spring and was to be completed by September 1, 1924.[22] Once the wall was in place, a portion of the 60-foot sand-hill extending east from the pier was literally "washed down", using old steam pumpers and fire hoses acquired from a Buffalo fire company, as well as horses pulling shovels to reclaim shallow land that was previously under water.[23] Crystal Beach employees completed this task.[24]

The Famous Ballroom

Late fall of this same year found the first excavations being started for the famous quarter-million-dollar Crystal Beach dance pavilion. Concrete work was to be completed and ready for the erection of structural steel by February 1, 1925, with the entire ballroom ready for opening no later than May 1. Failure to fulfill this contract would mean a loss of $100 per day by the contractors, Schultz Brothers Company of Brantford, Ontario.[25]

Hailed as one of the largest dance halls in North America, it was unique in its cantilever construction. This meant that there were no supporting pillars or posts in the middle of the dance floor, which was unusual for its day.[26] This 20,000 square-foot dance floor could easily hold 1,500 couples, at ten cents a dance or three dances for twenty-five cents.[27] Many of the well-known orchestras of the Big Band Era performed here, including Glenn Miller, Stan Kenton, Guy Lombardo, Les Brown, Woody Herman, Tommy and Jimmy Dorsey, and Ray McKinley, to name but a few.[28]

With the removal of a portion of the sand-hill, additional land became available to expand the Midway by 600 percent. This meant more rides and concessions could be added to the park.[29]

In 1926 construction began on the 96-foot-high Cyclone Roller Coaster, advertised as the "World's Largest, Fastest, Safest and Most Thrilling Ride" by its designer, Harry G. Traver. It was completed for the 1927 season at a cost of $176,000. Its construction absorbed 250 tons of structural, prefabricated steel, 20,000 board feet of British Columbia fir and several tons of spikes, screws and nails. A ride cost 20 cents and lasted 40 terrifying seconds. It was the only coaster known to have a nurse on duty at the unloading platform during its 20 years of operation, ending September 2, 1946.[30]

The Americana ceased operation in 1928, in part a consequence of the opening of the Peace Bridge the previous year, which made automobile travel to Crystal Beach much easier. [31]

Rival amusement park Erie Beach, in Fort Erie, closed for the last time on Labour Day, 1930, in part due to the Great Depression (1929 to 1939). Crystal Beach had gained the upper hand, with newer and more sophisticated rides. A provision of its sale was that Erie Beach could never again be used for the purpose of "public amusement". Some of the rides, games and other assets were then brought to Crystal Beach.[32]

Bankruptcy Filed

Crystal Beach filed for bankruptcy in 1931. This was a temporary setback, for two years later George Hall Sr., Charles Diebold and Charles Laube bought it from the bank. Reorganization took place and three firms emerged: The Crystal Beach Company Ltd. retained operating rights; The Crystal Beach Transit Company with George Hall Sr. as president ran the *Canadiana*; and the D.H.L. Company Ltd. owned the land.[33] This latter company's initials most likely stood for Diebold, Hall and Laube, its three owners. The two elder sons of George Hall Sr., Fillmore and Edward, became involved in the park's operation at this time. Youngest son George Jr. did not follow until 1948.[34]

George Sr. continued to improve the park. Even during the year bankruptcy was filed, roughly $65,000 was poured into the facility. Perhaps this caused the financial problems of the park that year. A new bathhouse was built, able to accommodate 10,000 bathers; the picnic grove was doubled in size; the parking space expanded by 50 per cent and another miniature golf course was added.[35]

The Laff-in-the-Dark was built in 1936, housed in what was previously home to the bowling alleys. The company responsible for the design of this "dark" ride was R.E. Chambers of Beaver Falls, Pennsylvania.[36] It is interesting to note that before 1932 this firm was known as the Traver Engineering Company, run by Harry Traver, designer of the famous Cyclone coaster.[37]

Ralph E. Chambers was one of the Traver Company engineers. Ralph bought his employer's company.[38] A brother of one of Traver's engineers, John Mitchell, was James T. Mitchell[39] a design engineer of the park whose brainchild was the Comet Roller Coaster. The Comet went into operation in 1948.[40]

The final year for the Cyclone was 1946. Old age, excessive maintenance costs and less public interest in the ride combined to seal its fate.[41] Ironically, the man who had been in charge of erecting the Cyclone was also in charge of dismantling it, namely Peter Cowan, superintendent of erection for The Standard Steel Company of Welland, Ontario.[42]

New Coaster

The Comet's cost of $125,000 was relatively low due to the fact that 60 per cent of the 300 tons of structural steel used in its construction came from its predecessor, the Cyclone. Two other factors which helped to keep expenses down were the cheap Canadian labor and the fact that the new steel was bought unfabricated, thus bent, cut, drilled, painted and assembled right on the site, ready for the park's opening on Decoration Day, 1948.[43]

The Comet occupied 800 feet along the park's promenade,[44] thus bringing an end to moonlit walks along the waterfront. This was only one of many changes that would occur during James Mitchell's tenure as assistant general manager of the park. The Midway was paved in 1939, with the power lines placed underground in 1946.[45] This era also found modernistic touches in evidence in the decorative scheme[46] throughout the famous two-million-dollar midway.[47] New rides at this time included the Rocket Ship, Auto Speedway, Auto Scooter and the Magic Carpet, which was a walk-through fun house.[48]

The 1950's brought about the decline of the dance hall; with the coming of the "rock and roll" era, small groups replaced the Big Bands all across North America, not just locally.[49]

Two Eras Come To An End

The *Canadiana* made its final trip between Buffalo and Crystal Beach at the end of the 1956 season. Rising operating costs, as well as the increased use of automobiles, helped to make the decision.[50] Chartered buses took over her duties, beginning with Canada Coach Lines Ltd., at lower rates.[51]

As dancing in the ballroom ended, Dexter's Roller Rink moved from its location beside the Giant coaster into the dance hall.[52] This was the third home for the roller rink. It was first located up on the sand-hill that was washed into the lake in 1924. Roller-skating lasted from the late 1950's until just before the fire of 1974.[53]

Until his death, George C. Hall Sr. was the president of the Crystal Beach Transit Company, with eldest son Fillmore as general manager, Edward as vice president and youngest son George Jr. as treasurer.[54] Fillmore followed his father as president after the latter's death until 1973, when he and his brother Edward retired from active management of Crystal Beach Park, giving over most of their responsibilities to their respective sons, Van and Bob.[55] Van worked primarily with his father at the Buffalo office as well as at the park itself, while Bob worked with his father in the direct operation of the park.[56]

Devastating Fire

A fire occurred in the dance hall in August 1974, originating in the Fantasyland attraction beneath the roller rink. Wax figures in the Hollywood Wax Museum, also located in the basement, melted, and the ballroom's maple flooring buckled.[57] Approximately half a million dollars was spent that winter to refurbish the damage caused by the fire. Another quarter-million dollars updated the ancient washrooms and moved the facilities to the main floor from the basement.[58]

The next year, 1975, a new restaurant called "The Big Top" opened in the renovated dance hall.[59] Beer and wine were served for the first time on the park premises.[60]

A pay-one-price admission of $5.50 to the park came into effect with the 1976 season.[61] This one price did not, however, include a ride on the famous Comet roller coaster. That would cost an extra 25 cents.[62]

The 60-foot-high water slide, Crown Mountain, built on the remaining natural sand -hill at the west end of the park, was ready late in 1978.[63]

Park In Receivership

In 1983 the park went into receivership. Ramsi Tick was brought in to manage the park under an agreement with the Canadian Imperial Bank of Commerce, who held it in receivership.[64] Tick was responsible for the return of a passenger excursion boat from Buffalo to Crystal Beach, namely the Miss Buffalo ll, running only on Thursdays.[65] Plus, Tick began a choice of admission fees to the park. You could pay one price for a full day of rides. Or you could pay a one-dollar admission fee to the park and then pay for each ride.[66]

The Backety-Back Scenic Railway Roller Coaster.
Harvey Holzworth Collection

The next year, in 1984, Edward Hall, Rudy Bonifacio, Joseph Biondolillo and J. Allen Bernel bought the park. The latter died after the arrangement was completed, so the remaining three owners bought Mr. Bernel's interest.[67] The famous ballroom was restored, opening once again for dancing on special evenings,[68] but with only half of the old dance floor. The north section that was destroyed by the fire in 1974[69] did not receive a new maple hardwood dance floor.

Carousel Sold

Always a popular ride, The Carousel was sold in December 1984 in an effort to raise needed capital to make improvements to the park. It had fallen into disrepair in later years, making the cost of restoration prohibitive.[70] It was dismantled and shipped to Fort Wayne, Indiana, for auction. Twenty-three horses, twenty-one other animals and two chariots were sold separately for close to $500,000 U.S. The top price paid for any one animal was $29,000 U.S. for the St. Bernard dog.[71]

The next year, in 1985, a seven-million-dollar renovation plan was announced. Completion date was set for 1988 in time for the park's 100th anniversary.[72] Schooner's Beach Club opened for the start of the 1987 season,

31

housed in the remodeled bathhouse.[73] The marina complex and pier restaurant, a large portion of the park's facelift, never came to be before its demise.

Park Closes

The gates closed for the last time on Labor Day, 1989. Declining attendance and increased costs were cited for this decision.[74]

An auction was held on site at the park on October 17, 1989, conducted by Norton Auctioneers of Michigan Inc., ironically the same company that auctioned off the Carousel just five years earlier. Anyone wishing to attend had to pay a $10 entrance fee in American funds. As well, everything sold had to be paid for in American funds. The weather conditions mirrored the mood of those in attendance – damp, cold and wet, a fitting ending never to be forgotten by all who braved the elements that final day.[75] The one-day sale earned more than one million dollars, in U.S. funds, of course![76] The Comet roller coaster sold for $210,000 to Charles Wood, owner of the Great Escape amusement park near Lake George, N.Y.[77] After being stored at his other park, Fantasy Island on Grand Island, N.Y., until the fall of 1993, it was moved to the Great Escape, where it was rebuilt, and has thrilled its many fans since the 1994 season.

Dismantling of the amusements and buildings began immediately after the auction and continued until the once-proud park was leveled, ending with the ballroom in June 1991.

New Owners

In the spring of 1990 the park changed ownership once more. Davis Tiburzi and Bob Gelder, Williamsville, N.Y. businessmen, along with Al Lacavera, a Welland, Ontario lawyer, took possession of the property.[78]

Unsuccessful attempts were made by numerous area residents to keep the park land from being developed for residential use. They had hoped that it could have been designated for a passive park in order to keep the land for public use, as this was one of the last pieces of lakefront property available for such a purpose.[79]

Official ground-breaking ceremonies took place in August 1992 for the Crystal Beach Tennis and Yacht Club.[80] Three houses were under construction in 1993. An in-ground pool and a tennis court were added in 1994. By mid-summer of 1995, 18 single-family homes were either completed or were under construction. This development has continued to the present day.

Footnotes

1. Francis Petrie, "Crystal Beach Was Religious Colony", *Niagara Falls Review*, January 1970.
2. Peter C. Andrews, "Crystal Beach First Opened in 1888 as Religious Assembly Ground", *Buffalo Courier-Express*, July 8, 1952
3. Cathy A. Herbert and John Burtniak, eds., *Scenes of Greater Fort Erie, Ridgeway*, Ont.: by the Editors, 1989, p.1
4. Herbert and Burtniak, pp.14, 18.
5. C.J. Pilkey, Crystal Beach Guide, Crystal Beach: C.J. Pilkey, 1922, p.1
6. Cathy Herbert Collection, Crystal Beach Steamboat & Ferry Co. stock, 1892.
7. Andrews.
8. Herbert and Burtniak, p.1.
9. Andrews.
10. Herbert and Burtniak, p.17.
11. Francis Petrie, "Crystal Beach: The Coney Island of Canada", *Niagara Falls Review*, ca 1971.
12. Floyd Baker, *Short History & Description of the Canadiana, Prospectus for the S.S. Canadiana Preservation Society Inc.*, Buffalo, N.Y., 1993, introduction.
13. "Crystal Beach Opens Saturday", Fort Erie *Times*, May 1910.
14. "Crystal Beach Notes", Fort Erie *Times*, May 19, 1910.
15. Petrie.
16. "Crystal Beach Notes".
17. "Crystal Beach Opens Saturday"
18. Herbert and Burtniak, p.18.
19. "Crystal Beach Changes Hands", Fort Erie *Times*, March 28, 1924.
20. Paul Jayes, "Crystal Beach Started With Picnic Grove", *Buffalo Courier-Express*, May 26, 1971.
21. "Crystal Beach Changes Hands".
22. Cathy Herbert Collection, Specifications for Sea Wall, Crystal Beach, Ontario, March 12. 1924.
23. Personal interview with Helen Rebstock, 1989.
24. Personal interview with Edward Hall, October 1989.
25. Cathy Herbert Collection, Specifications for Dance Pavilion for Buffalo & Crystal Beach Corporation, October 1, 1924.
26. Personal interview with Edward Hall, October 1989.
27. George Ono, "Crystal Beach Ballroom Will Be Rebuilt – Owner", *Niagara Falls Review*, Fall, 1974.
28. Cathy Herbert Collection, various Big Band posters.
29. Jayes.
30. Richard Munch, *Harry G. Traver: Legends of Terror, Mentor, Ohio*: Amusement Park Books Inc., 1982, pp. 78, 85.
31. Herbert and Burtniak, p.14.
32. Ibid., pp.26, 27.
33. Ibid., p.1.
34. Personal interview with Edward Hall, October 1989.
35. "Crystal beach Opens May 28", *The Billboard*, May 28, 1931.
36. Cathy Herbert Collection, correspondence between Crystal Beach Company and R.E. Chambers, 1935 and 1936.
37. Munch, p.14.
38. Ibid.
39. Ibid.
40. Art Dogan, "Giant Crystal Beach Coaster To Give Most Thrilling Ride", *Buffalo Evening News*, January 9, 1948.
41. Munch, p.85.

42 "Cyclone Coaster Is Being Dismantled: Beach Thrill-ride Will Be Replaced", *Buffalo Evening News*, September 13, 1946.

43 Dogan

44 Ibid.

45 Paul Rubin, Ninety-nine Years of Crystal Beach", *Amusement Park Journal*, Natrona Heights, Pa.: Charles J. Jacques Jr., February 1987, p.12.

46 "Readying for Revelry", *Buffalo Courier-Express Pictoral*, May 25, 1947.

47 1949 *Manual & Guide, Handbook of the Industry*, 6th Edition, Chicago Ill.: The National Association of Amusement Parks, Pools and Beaches, 1949.

48 "Readying for Revelry".

49 Personal interview with Fred Truckenbrodt, May 1994.

50 "Steamer Canadiana Will Run To Crystal Beach No More", *Buffalo Evening News*, November 27, 1956.

51 "18,400,000 Passengers Later, Canadiana Calls It Quits", *Buffalo Evening News*, November 28, 1956.

52 Personal interview with Edward Hall, October 1989.

53 Personal interview with Gertrude Dexter, May 1994.

54 Jayes.

55 Herbert and Burtniak, p.1.

56 Personal interview with Van Hall, May 1994.

57 "Crystal Beach Fire Closes Attractions", *Niagara Falls Review*, August 16, 1974.

58 Personal interview with Van Hall, May 1994.

59 "Spruced Up Amusement Park Offers New Rides, Restaurants", *Niagara Falls Review*, May 1975.

60 Personal interview with Van Hall, May 1994.

61 Rick Mauro, "New Prices, New Rides", *Fort Erie Times-Review*, June 9, 1976.

62 Personal interview with Van Hall, May 1994.

63 Ray Dearlove, "Crystal Midway Adds Riding Gear", *Buffalo Courier-Express*, May 1978.

64 Herbert and Burtniak, p.1.

65 Mike Vogel, "Dry Spell Ends for Crystal Beach Boat", *Buffalo Evening News*, June 6, 1983.

66 Advertisement for Crystal Beach Park, *Buffalo Evening News*, July 31, 1983.

67 Herbert and Burtniak, p.1.

68 "Crystal Ballroom Opens With Concerts July 6", Fort Erie *Times-Review*, June 27, 1984.

69 Personal interview with Van Hall, May 1994.

70 Robert J. McCarthy, "Plan To Sell Carousel Spurs Cry of 'Hold Your Horses' ", *Buffalo Evening News*, November 11, 1984.

71 Robert J. McCarthy, "Auction of Crystal Beach Carousel Rounds Up Nearly $500,000", *Buffalo Evening News*, December 15, 1984.

72 "Marina Is Flagship to $7 Million Facelift", *Guardian Express*, December 11, 1985.

73 "Crystal Beach Adding Pub, New Ride", *Buffalo Evening News*, May 21, 1987.

74 "Crystal Beach To Cease Operations As Amusement Park", Fort Erie *Times-Review*, August 26, 1989.

75 Personal recollections of Cathy Herbert.

76 "Speculation Is Over: Crystal Beach Park Sold", unknown newspaper, May 1990.

77 Mike Vogel, "There Were No Big Dips In Bidding For Comet Coaster", *The Buffalo News*, October 18, 1989.

78 Personal interview with Phil McGuire, May 1994.

79 Personal interview with Janet Truckenbrodt, May 1994.

80 Mike Sturman, "Park Transformation Official", Fort Erie *Times-Review*, August 11, 1992.

"...she really choked."
David

In 1948 I was a 7-year-old shoeshine boy who worked on Broadway in Buffalo, New York. I charged 25 cents for a shoeshine. When I made 4 dollars I'd go down to the Crystal Beach Boat, buy a ticket and sail over to the park, all by myself. I would have a ball and sail back in the evening.

Years later I told my mother what I used to do and she really choked. She had no idea that I traveled that far from home. Too bad kids today can't do something like that. It was a great experience.

"...supervised the building of the new Comet..."
James T. Mitchell

James T. Mitchell, who had worked for Harry Traver and had helped to build the "Cyclone" ride in 1927, went to work at Crystal Beach in 1940 as park superintendent. He supervised the building of the new Comet coaster with an in-house crew. Stretching over 800 feet long along the waterfront, the ride would, in part, occupy the promenade on the lake side of the ballroom. This would be a loss to dancers who liked to sit out there on hot nights.

"... the smell of gasoline and Old Spice aftershave."
Trudy M. Mitchell

I am the grand daughter of James T. Mitchell, the design engineer who created the Comet roller coaster that replaced the cyclone coaster in 1948. His eldest son, my father, is James L. Mitchell. My father and my mother, at 18 years of age, were the first humans to ride the coaster on its test run. According to family legend, sand bags in the other coaster seats accompanied mom and dad. How's that for courage!

I spent many ecstatic childhood hours at Crystal Beach at my grandparents' home and at the park. I remember hopping on the back of my grandfather's tri-wheeler and riding to the park on the back foot-stand, my arms wrapped tightly about his neck. To this day, I equate the smell of gasoline and Old Spice aftershave with perfect happiness.

At the age of two, the family history also has it that I refused to leave the Carousel until my poor mother had nearly passed out after 13 consecutive rides. The Laff in the Dark, the Fun House and the man who used to sit in the

Comet's first drop is the highest.
Courtesy of Buffalo State College, Courier Collection

tower waiting for women to walk over the air vent with full skirts on - what memories! Thanks for the invoking of such wonderful memories!

"My dad walked the tracks of both coasters each day."
Jim Mitchell

Yes, my wife and I were in the front seat of the coaster when they were testing the coaster. There were sand bags in the other seats. I had faith in my dad's ability to design coasters.

My dad walked the tracks of both coasters each day. I also remember my dad going all over the world to get the right lumber for the track and supports for the coaster.

Dad's wife had several games in the park. On our vacation my wife and I would count tickets and pennies from the different pitch-penny games.

I remember the dance hall being used as a roller rink in the late 1940's.

"Boy was she in some serious trouble..."
P. Laborce

French fries in a cone-shaped cup, drenched in vinegar. Thank you Crystal Beach for a classic snack that lives on. One of my favourite old family stories is of my great Auntie Irene running to catch the boat back to Buffalo and losing one of her shoes as she made the jump for the boat. Boy was she in some serious trouble when she arrived home that night.

"My father stood at the top of the Crystal Ballroom steps with a machine gun protecting half a million dollars during the riot."
Fred Truckenbrodt

I was born in 1919 at 3925 Alexandra Road, Crystal Beach, Ontario, Canada. My grandmother's family goes back so far in America that we can't really trace them. They were Climenhages and they came up from Pennsylvania after the American Revolution 1776-1783, as United Empire Loyalists who opposed the revolution. They wanted Canada and America to be a united country.

But my grandfather came from Alsace-Lorraine in Germany to escape the Franco-Prussian War, 1870-1871. His parents were Quakers like my grandmother's people and they were pacifists. So granddad's parents got him to Holland and on a boat to America and Buffalo where his uncle, Mr. Schmidt, was the postmaster general at the time.

Granddad was a painter apprentice in Germany where the training was intensive. Granddad taught his two sons the same trade. When he got to Buffalo he worked on the boats as a painter from March until fall. Buffalo was the Queen of the lakes in the grain industry. Granddad would sail to Fort William and Port Arthur now Thunder Bay. From Duluth, Minnesota he returned to Buffalo.

Granddad told of the Indians who would load the boats. They would carry the bags of grain on the ship, not like today with the self-loaders. The Indians were paid in whiskey and were not paid until the boat was pulling away from the dock. They did this because the Indians got drunk so fast that there was a problem getting the boat underway if the whiskey was paid too soon. Granddad said that the Indians had a problem with alcohol because their employers made them that way.

Granddad spent the winters in Buffalo and one winter Mr. Le Jeune asked him to come to Port Colborne, Ontario where he could work all winter on a boat that was wintered there. At nineteen he arrived in Port Colborne, worked and traveled the area, visiting Ridgeway and the hotel and the dining room that was run by my grandmother and her family. He asked my grandmother's sister if she would go buggy riding with him on Sunday. Her mother agreed on condition that Janette would accompany them as a chaperone. My grandmother Janette was born with a club foot, which in those days they couldn't do anything about so she wore a heavy sole about four inches thick on the one foot for the rest of her life. Since she wasn't considered marriageable, she was sent along as a chaperone. The following Sunday my grandfather asked Janette to go for a buggy ride and her sister had to go along as the chaperone.

For the next ten years the sisters hardly spoke to each other because granddad asked Janette to marry him and she said, "Yes!" They were married in Ridgeway in 1875. My grandmother was much younger than my grandfather and she outlived him by many years.

Then Fred Truckenbrodt and Janette Climenhage (grandparents) married and settled down on Disher Street in Ridgeway and the children started right away. The kids all went to school on the corner of Disher Street and Ridge Road. That is where my father went to school.

One day my aunt Grace came home from school with tears in her eyes. She was the third daughter and said that she would not go back to school. My grandfather asked, "Why not?" And she said, "Because they are teasing me about my name." At that point they were Drybreads, Fred Drybread. My grandfather had anglicized Truckenbrodt into the English meaning, Drybread. So he said, "Well if they are going to do that Grace, we'll just change your name back to what it should be, Truckenbrodt." He said, "If you go upstairs to my trunk in the attic you will see my name on it and that's going to be your name henceforth." Aunty Grace said that she had a terrible time for three days trying to learn Truckenbrodt because it was difficult compared to Drybread. We still have the trunk up in my barn at home, an old leather trunk with wallpaper lining.

I think that I know the origin of that name. There is a tradition in Europe that if you sell bread from a store but the bread is not baked there in the store then that is a Truckenbrodt. The store owner buys the bread wholesale from bakeries and retails the bread at his store.

Anyway, they were living on Disher Street. Aunt Ida's diary starts at 1898 in Ridgeway and ends up at what they called The Berlin Farm, which is Windmill Point, on the Windmill Point Road directly across from the quarries. On the farm they took in boarders who dug the quarries and we have pictures of them at the house. The property has been developed today. But when I was a child my mother used to say, "There's the Six Mile Creek where your father and I used to spoon at night on the bank of the creek when we were on the farm."

All the family came home to that farm because there was a Windmill Point Station on the train. All the girls who had gone to Buffalo to work would come home with their husbands or boyfriends on the weekend and the farmhouse was bursting at the seams. Cousin Ethel has said that on Sunday there'd be 25 to 30 people who would sit down to a meal. There was always a white linen tablecloth, white linen napkins, the best china and sterling silver. Ethel said that it was always a joy to come to the farm because that was the way that it should be. That was in the summer. In the winter they would be gone.

My mother said that at times someone would miss the train so they'd just walk the railroad track, a distance of six to seven miles and think nothing of it as a girl or a woman. That was life then.

My grandfather farmed and Aunt Jenny said that as Uncle Jim ploughed she would sit up in a tree as a little girl and watch him plough back and forth until it came her turn.

Aunt Jenny and my father would work on the farm together. They both had horses. Then in the evening they would go out and play Bill Coty games riding bareback on their horses in the fields. Aunt Jenny said that my father

Lincoln Hotel
Cathy Herbert Collection

would imitate Bill Coty. While riding the horse Dad could swing underneath the horse and come up on the other side. While riding the horse he could also slide off the back of the horse while holding its tail, turn a handspring and get back up on the horse.

This was a large family and from oldest to youngest consisted of: Abby, Florence, Grace, Uncle Jim, Ida, Louise, my father Charlie, and the baby Aunt Jenny. There were seven years between the rest of the kids and Charlie and Jenny.

Aunt Louise would come home from Buffalo on the train. Ed Buck was the conductor on the train and this is my grandfather's story. Aunty Louise made up to Uncle Ed and brought him home. When he saw Aunt Abbie, he didn't want anything more to do with Aunt Lousie so he took after Aunt Abbie. They fell in love and wanted to get married. My grandfather said, "No". So they got married secretly in Buffalo, came home and told the family.

Uncle Ed and Abbie took off for California in 1901 about the time of the gold rush there. But they returned in two years and opened a combined laundry and barbershop across from the Ridgeway Library. The first summer it was just a tent with a barber pole in front of it. The next summer they had a shanty on the corner where the main entrance to Crystal Beach Park was situated on Erie and Ridge Road. They bought more property because they could see the potential of Crystal Beach. It was starting to boom. Around 1904 they bought the property for the Lincoln Hotel.

Not long after that, around 1907 or 1908 my grandfather and grandmother Truckenbrodt sold the farm at Windmill Point and they moved to Crystal Beach as well. And they bought property. They owned all the property on Erie Road from the corner of Ridgeway Road and halfway to Derby. Until recently, Aunt Jenny owned three houses on Erie Road. My grandfather died there in the New Yorker Cottage in 1917.

My father and mother, Charlie and Helen were married in 1914 and lived in a little cottage behind the New Yorker until they bought our house on Alexandra Road in 1917.

Aunt Abbie and Uncle Ed built the Lincoln Hotel and it was everything. It started as a general store at 156 Lincoln Rd. in downtown Crystal Beach. But it was a general store with a laundry behind and a barbershop on the side and a dining room on the other side where you could go in and have sandwiches and tea. It was an all-purpose building, one of the few places in Crystal Beach that was open all winter. Summer businesses were abundant but they were closed in the winter.

It was because of the Lincoln Hotel that my father met my mother. Mom was from Buffalo and she went to work for some wealthy people named Chesters at Point Abino. They came to the general store to buy their food. Often they would phone the order for groceries. My father would take the horse and buggy and deliver the groceries to Point Abino. He'd drop them off and pick up the dirty laundry from that house and three days later deliver the clean laundry.

The Chesters had a very pretty upstairs maid who my father started to make eyes at during one of his deliveries. Soon there was a romance between the upstairs maid and the delivery boy.

As the population grew in Crystal Beach there was a need for a post office. Aunt Ida Truckenbrodt became the postmistress of Crystal Beach. There was a little counter on the side of the general store and a little enamel sign that that said Post Office. Stamps were sold and mail was dropped. Aunt Jenny and my father would take the mail in a bag in a horse and buggy and deliver it every day to the Canadian National train in Ridgeway. That was another one of their jobs. Aunt Jenny had all the fun jobs and had such a good time doing them.

Then Uncle Ed became the Treasurer of Crystal Beach when it became a village in the 1920's and held that position until the day that he died. Plus, Uncle Ed became a justice of the peace and sat as a judge in court when the police laid a charge. But Uncle Ed kept his Treasurer's Office in his own building, which was a few steps away from the fire hall and municipal building where they had the jail. The first jail was in the old stone building on the Circle. But later they had three cells in the municipal building.

Nothing serious ever happened. But in the 1920's and 30's there would be a hundred thousand people here on the weekend. That meant that there would be a drunk or two and a disorderly person once in a while. The police could bring someone before my uncle on a charge because my uncle was always there. My uncle would have to get out of bed at 2 a.m. to declare someone disorderly so that the police could lock him up for the night. Then some people wanted to get married in the middle of the night.

Then when I'd be walking home from school I'd run into Aunt Jenny and her dog. Jenny had a basket over her arm and she was walking over to the jail with food for the prisoner. From day one the hotel also fed the prisoners and Aunt Jenny delivered the meals of homemade bread, meat, homemade pies and a thermos of hot tea. The prisoners ate better in jail than at home.

All these things were going on so that the hotel was really a fantastic place. Almost everyone in Crystal Beach was expected at some time during the day to stop at the hotel for a cup of tea, a glass of milk, pancake or whatever was available. My aunt baked at least twelve loaves of homemade bread per day along with six elderberry, peach, pear or apple pies as well. She had pie racks and a free slice of pie was offered to anyone who came in for a cup of tea. It was an open-house most of the time.

In the hotel they had 12 bedrooms upstairs and a large dining room and a very large kitchen. Plus they had their own living quarters with my uncle's office to the side. In the summer they had the same people come back to the hotel. For example, there was a Dr. Calahan who was a dentist in Buffalo. He and his family would always come for the first two weeks of July for many years.

In the winter, the rooms would be empty and so they carried on the tradition of boarding the Windmill Point quarrymen. When they built the Crystal Beach Ballroom in 1925, at that time the largest ballroom in the world, the hotel boarded about 50 workers for two years during construction. Aunt Jenny and Ida would take their dog each day and visit the construction site. Here they would watch the construction workers wash away the massive sand dunes with powerful water hoses. Then Jenny and Ida watched the workers erect the steel where the sand dunes once stood. This was a unique ballroom. Not like the big ballroom in Cleveland where every twenty feet they had a post and the dancers kept banging into a post. The Crystal Ballroom had one and a half acres of giant ballroom floor without any posts. This was unique.

I went to work in the ballroom taking tickets when I was twelve. We called it working the ropes. Dances were five cents a ticket when I started working there. At the end of a dance we would sweep the people off the back of the dance floor with these long ropes that stretched across the floor. The new people would come onto the floor from the front and dance to the next song. We had to see that all the people were off the floor because a new dance would cost you another five cents and you gave up your ticket at the front. A dance was three minutes long.

Between 12 and 20 years of age I worked at Crystal Beach and I can't describe how wonderful that was for me. There were two bands that played on band nights, a Canadian and an American band. In my time it was Bert Niosi who played the Palais Royale in Toronto in the winter and Crystal Beach in the summer. I knew Johnny, Joe and Bert Niosi and my sister babysat Bert's kids when she was a girl. Joe Niosi was in the airforce with me so we used to see each other in Ottawa. He was the number one airforce band during the war.

Harold Austin was the orchestra that came over on the Crystal Beach Boat from Buffalo. With musician-union rules, there had to be a Canadian band in the Ballroom or an American band couldn't play. So the Canadian band started at 8 p.m. and the boat arrived at 9:15 and at 9:30 Harold Austin played until 11p.m. Then Bert Niosi would play until midnight. Harold Austin left Buffalo at eight o'clock every night, seven days a week from Decoration Day until Labor Day. And all the people in Buffalo who had worked all day would come out and dance to an 18 piece orchestra on this beautiful maple dance floor on the back deck of the Canadiana on a hot summer's night, moon over water and then land at Crystal Beach. After a short walk to the Crystal Ballroom they could dance the night away and then get back on the boat and dance their way back to Buffalo until fifteen minutes past midnight when the boat landed. I saw the Harold Austin orchestra come down the covered walk from the bridge with their bass fiddles and their saxophones. They looked like the Buffalo Symphony Orchestra coming out after a concert.

Crystal Beach in the summer revolved around the boat, much like Martha's Vineyard or Nantucket. In the early days, everybody came on the boat, 3500 at a time because they did not have cars in the 1920's and the depression during the 1930's. If you had a car you would not drive it to Crystal Beach. But everyone in Buffalo could afford the street car to the dock on Commercial Street and take the hour boat-ride to Crystal Beach and be there for a day or the evening, have a swim and dance until you dropped. These were everyday people. This was affordable mass culture, new to the world and available to everyone not just the rich people.

Then there were the groups of young friends who would form and go to the beach in the afternoon and to the Ballroom at night. Then big name bands started to arrive at the Ballroom. Almost all summer, every Saturday night we'd see a big name band. My favorite was Jimmy Dorsey and I was absolutely in love with Helen O'Connell. I had all the old 78 records that I played on this scratchy Victrola. So I met Helen O'Connell and Bob Everly and had them sign my posters. I was so thrilled. Then Benny Goodman, Tommy Dorsey, Larry Clinton, Louise King performed there and a host of other people.

Then we had a terrible time one Labor Day. I was working the door of the Ballroom and Artie Shaw was coming. Each year one of the big bands would become the band of the year. For example there was Tommy Dorsey with Frank Sinatra one year and Benny Goodman and Glenn Miller during other years. Then the Artie Shaw frenzy hit. And I can remember saying to the girl who I was going with as she stood beside me at the Ballroom door: "Can you imagine? What a way to finish the summer! Artie Shaw!" We were just so thrilled! Well Artie Shaw was late. Poor old Bert Niosi was playing and playing and playing well into Artie Shaw's time. Artie was a real eccentric and had trouble wherever he played. He caused trouble with a custom's officer and Artie was held up at Canadian Customs. They wouldn't let him enter Canada.

Finally he arrived at 10:10 and he was supposed to perform at 9 p.m. He no sooner starts to play and union rules say that at 11 p.m. he must take a break. And he did until 11:30. The patrons paid ten dollars per person to hear Artie Shaw. He arrives late and stops playing soon after he started. Ten dollars then would be like big bucks today. Artie was upstairs in an argument over his wages for that night. They were not going to pay him for the time that he was late. In the meantime the patrons downstairs rioted—they went wild! They had had enough. They tore all the microphones off the stand, they trashed the band instruments and then broke 3000 windows in the Crystal Ballroom. It was a terror. Then Artie Shaw wouldn't come down because of the riot and he remained marooned upstairs. It was a disaster.

On top of all this it was Labor Day, the biggest day of the year for cash and the upstairs office had all the money for that day in the safe, over half a million dollars. My father was ordered to stand at the top of the stairs with a machine gun because the riot might spread to the upper offices and all the money could be stolen. When the police arrived they gave him the gun and told him if the rioters started upstairs to give one warning and then to shoot. But the people were not interested in coming upstairs. They were rioting because Artie Shaw had given them a dirty deal. They didn't get what they had paid for. So the Crystal Beach Company announced next day on the radio that everyone who came into the Buffalo office would get his or her money back.

My Dad was the painting contractor for the Crystal Beach Company. On Decoration Day, the Fourth of July and Labor Day, the Company asked their men to come in to work and act as security. My Dad was sitting on a chair at the top of the stairs in the Crystal Ballroom when the police gave him the machine gun. The year was 1941. The Japanese attacked Pearl Harbor in December of that year and the USA entered World War Two. Canada had entered World War Two in 1939.

In the winter we would all go to Shea's Buffalo to hear the bands. I heard Harry James there and Glenn Miller several times. When you went to the theater, you just listened. When you went to Crystal Beach you danced to the music and that was wonderful.

Bert Niosi was like Guy Lombardo. They both started in London Ontario. Bert could play nineteen instruments but was essentially a trumpet player. He was the big band of southern Ontario, Canada.

Let me tell you more about the Canadiana. At first there was the Americana and the Canadiana. The Americana was sold to carry excursions from New York City to Rye New York. This boat was sold because cars were more plentiful and the Canadiana could handle the boat passengers to and from Crystal Beach. In June, the Canadiana was a beautiful white sight with three thousand passengers as it docked in Crystal Beach. You could hear the orchestra playing. The whole village was tuned into the boat because it came every two hours. The first boat arrived at 11 a.m., then 1:15 p.m., 3:30, 6:15, 8:15 and eleven o'clock. When the boat was secured to the dock and before anyone embarked or disembarked, the boat would blow its whistle and we could hear it all over Crystal Beach. People would say that the boat is in, it must be eleven o'clock.

When I went to college for 4 years I had to work two jobs. I worked the Ballroom and caught the ropes on the boat when it docked. With two jobs I could afford to go to college. The dock job meant as well that I had to clean the beach by hand. I was a real beachcomber in my day at Crystal Beach. I got up at four o'clock in the morning and picked up every single piece of paper and any kind of garbage that was on the beach all the way from Bay Beach to the Crystal Beach dock. That would take me three to four hours.

Then I went up onto the dock. There I swept the dock clean until the boat came in at eleven o'clock. That's when they threw me the lines from the Canadiana. If you have ever watched a boat come in, there's a tiny guide rope that they throw to shore. That guide rope is a quarter inch thick and is attached to a giant two-inch cable that I hauled up and secured to the mooring post buttons anchored at the dock. I met every boat until 6:30 p.m. The night watchman took the night shift.

I'd go home, have dinner and then report to work the Ballroom from eight o'clock until midnight that night. I was up at four the next morning for seven days a week except that the ballroom didn't dance on Sunday night. The Crystal Beach Boat danced but the Crystal Ballroom did not.

Lake Erie has some terrible storms. During the worst storms the Canadiana continued to sail. Lake Erie being a shallow lake can deliver a vicious storm in just a few minutes with massive crashing waves that are as high as a house. In severe weather the captain could not get the boat close enough to the dock to throw the line to me. That's when he would steer the boat so that he rammed the dock with the front of the boat. Then they would throw me the line off the front of the boat and I'd secure the cable on the mooring post. And the cables made such an awesome noise that you wondered if the boat would be safe.

I had nightmares about the boat not stopping and then floundering on the beach. I had seen a picture of one of the earlier boats that had beached in a storm. I'd wake up in the middle of the night in a panic because I saw myself miss the rope and the boat was beached. It was my entire fault!

Because of my hours, the only time that I could do anything was between 1:30 and 3:30 p.m. I'd go home for lunch and have a nap. All in the family worked. My mother sold tickets at the Park, my father was painting there as well and my sister had a job. I did not set an alarm for my nap. I awoke with the sound of the 3:30 boat whistle arriving at the dock where I was supposed to be catching a line. What a panic! There I was on the bed with no one to catch the ropes. I would be fired. The police will charge me with a serious offence. My college days would be finished.

With luck, it was a very calm day and I learned later that the first mate jumped off the boat onto the dock and secured the cable to the mooring post. He told me later that they did not report me because they did not want me to get into trouble. But they teased me for the rest of the summer about how I was too drunk that day to report for work.

On Sunday when I didn't have to go to the Ballroom, I would jump on the boat at 6:30 p.m. after I tossed the rope on board. The captain would let me steer the Canadiana all the way to Buffalo. The captain had a son as well and the captain used to say that they were proud of me that I was making something of myself by going to college and not just sitting around. It was wonderful to be on the top deck and see the lights of Buffalo appear in late August. Then I would eat my dinner down in the sailor's mess.

The purser invited me to see Crystal Beach from his place on the boat on the return trip. It was dark already. This was a most beautiful sight. The roller coasters had lights, the ballroom was lit up, the domes glistened and at that point they had an eighty-foot tower beside the dock with neon tubes that glowed in the dark. You could see the rides moving with all their lights while the band played down below me on the boat. An unforgettable sight and sound.

The Cyclone Roller Coaster was a desperate ride. It was vicious. It did figure eights and loop the loops and went 60 miles per hour into hairpin turns. You had to be a real dare- devil to ride it. Mind you three people were killed on it when they sat up in the chair rather than staying down. They sat on the back of the seat instead of under the guardrail. They were not aware of the danger. As they'd rise up and over a very sharp turn, they'd didn't turn. They just kept going straight.

There was a friend of my father, Ray Sherk, who got a taste of the Cyclone. There is a picture of the people coming off the boat wearing their white straw-hat boaters in the 1920's. Everyone wore a boater as did Ray Sherk. Ray was from Silver Creek, New York and when he arrived my dad teased him by saying, "Come on, you're so big and brave. Are you big and brave enough to ride the Cyclone?" Ray said, "Yes." There was a place to leave your hat when you rode the Cyclone. Ray refused to hang his hat saying, "This hat came from New York City and it cost way too much for me to leave it on a Cyclone hat rack." So Ray took his hat with him on the Cyclone and held it in his hands during the ride. When the ride was finished, Ray no longer had a white hat. Instead he had what looked like bits of popcorn in his hands. His hat was crushed to bits from squeezing when he went around those hairpin turns.

That Cyclone was on the east side of the Ballroom. That ride made such a racket, along with the screams of terrified roller coasters, that we had to keep the doors closed on that side of the Ballroom. There was such a racket that we couldn't hear the orchestra play. That dancehall was designed so that all sides of the room could be open to the cooler lake air in the hot weather.

Eight of us worked in the ballroom. We always wore uniforms, grey flannel pants with navy blue blazers, plus shirt and tie with white buck shoes. At 7:45 p.m. the eight of us would go over to the Cyclone and ride for free. They would say, "Here come the dance hall boys." We'd all go to the front of the Cyclone and sit two by two. And I did that every night for about two summers. It never lost its interest because it was such an exciting ride.

The Dance Hall Boys.
Cathy Herbert Collection

At eight o'clock, they used to line us up in the Ballroom as if we in the army. Then Frank Dumont, the drum major would shout left, right, left, right and we would parade from the front of the bandstand through the ballroom and then circle around until each of us had been left at our work station. It was like the changing of the guard. On a busy night we'd have six hundred people watching this procession while they waited to get onto the dance floor.

There were eight gates at our work stations so that people could get out onto the dance floor. We had boxes with crushers in them. It was like going into the theater. There were iron pipe channels and the people would be lined up in these channels and you'd take tickets with both hands. In the theater they used to rip the tickets in half. But we had to crush the tickets in each hand and the couple would come through. It took quite a while to learn the crushing trick. But you had to break them in two and then drop them in the box. There was a ship's wheel on the front of the box. When you spun the ship's wheel, there was a grinder on the bottom of the box and that grinder made confetti out of the tickets. We used the confetti on carnival night. We'd have buckets of this stuff in baskets up at the ceiling and we'd let it float down over the people who were dancing.

During the depression of the 1930's we'd try all sorts of things to keep people coming to the dance hall and Tuesday night was carnival night. In the afternoons, four of us would inflate 3000 balloons by mouth and hang them from the ceiling. There were no helium tanks in those days. Then everyone who came through for the first dance got a roll of serpentine, those paper streamers that you throw by hand. Later on, people received confetti. In the balloons there were prize tickets for floor lamps, folding chairs, pocket radios etc for the lucky people who broke the balloon with the prize tickets. It was great fun when the balloons came down because everyone was chasing and breaking balloons for the prizes.

Then we had spot dances on Thursday night and we'd darken the whole ballroom. I often ran the spotlight which consisted of a single white spot. I would glide this white spot over the people while they danced. When the music stopped so did the spot and the winner got a nice prize like a chest of silver-ware or a set of dishes. I had a lot of fun with that spotlight.

Another ride that was fun was the Old Mill. You sat in a boat that traveled through a canal inside a building that was very dark. You were supposed to be able to kiss in there. The Old Mill came here from Erie Beach when it closed. During the ride, a ghost or skeleton would jump out at you. But there were pretty scenes as well such as palm trees and crocodiles.

That tower near the dock that I mentioned was originally the airplane ride. There were four giant airplanes suspended on chains that would seat about eight people. These planes would swing far out on the end of their chains from the revolving central tower. Near the shore you thought that you were flying your plane over water. When that ride broke down they sold off the airplanes, put neon on the tower and built a garden at the base of the tower. That garden became a pretty place to go and rest.

There were the Tumblebugs, the HEYDEY and the Waterscooters, those little boats with rubber bumpers and you'd go around bumping everyone with them. The auto scooters were little cars that you bumped into other cars. The Fun House was replaced by the penny arcade. You would go up to the third floor in the Fun House and come sliding down to ground level by way of a circular slide that deposited you into the bottom of what they called the Sugar Bowl. The slide actually went outside the building so that on the way down you could see the trees and an overview of the Park. Then the slide re-entered the building. That bowl was about nine feet high, fourteen feet wide and made up of circular oak boards that were waxed. You were trapped at the bottom of it and had to keep trying to get up and out. If you couldn't get out, an attendant would throw you a rope and pull you out.

Then there were the crazy mirrors in the Fun House. They had twenty or thirty of them that made you fat or skinny or wobbly or any number of bizarre forms.

FUN HOUSE.
Photo by and courtesy of Alfred F. Sagon-King

The barrel was also in the Fun House, much like a slippery floor. It was a complete barrel that kept rolling. If you got in it and sat down then the barrel would roll you half way up its inside and you would slide down and then roll half way up again. It never stopped rolling. Kids would get in it and keep walking up one side of it as it continued to roll in one place. There were as many as fifty kids in the barrel at one time.

During the depression in the 1930's, we had friends from Buffalo named Whitlinger and they had a son named Fred too. He was thirteen and I was twelve. We would swim at the beach all day and at night we were given ten cents each. One night we would spend that money in the Fun House and the next night we went roller skating all night for ten cents. If we were tempted and spent our ten cents on a waffle or ice cream then we would sit in the balcony of the Ballroom, listen to the music and watch people dance. At nine o'clock we would have to leave. We did this all summer.

At first the rides cost five cents, then ten cents, then three for a quarter, then twenty five cents a ride and we thought that this was horrendous and today (1985) the Comet roller coaster is almost a dollar. But there are still lineups to ride the coaster.

I loved the Wild Mouse but it is gone. We loved the little roller coaster for kids, two and three year olds. The highest hill was eight feet and the little kids loved it.

HEYDEY - Comet 1965.
Rick Herbert Collection

Mr. Hall's story is interesting. He used to come over from Buffalo on the Crystal Beach Boat with a peanut wagon just like the old fashioned Italian people who would sell peanuts and chestnuts. Hall sold peanuts and popcorn on the boat on the way over, sold all day at the Park and then sold on the last boat home at night. He made enough money that he built a permanent candy concession at the Park where he made Hall's Suckers. Then he built another concession where he made Hall's Candy Kisses.

During the depression the Crystal Beach Company went broke around 1931 and went into receivership with the bank. Hall had made enough money from his business that he bought the Crystal Beach Company and the whole Park for almost nothing, two hundred thousand dollars. No one had any money in the depression. He also bought the Crystal Beach Boat and the dock in Buffalo for twenty five thousand dollars. Then he bought the beach attached to the Crystal Beach Amusement Park. That's when Halls became the single family owner of the whole thing.

The Crystal Beach Boat was officially called the Canadiana. It was docked in Buffalo in the harbor at the foot of Commercial Street, where it was laid up during the winter.

Crystal Beach itself and the Park were founded by John Evangelist Rebstock, originally as a Chautauqua. This was a tent city that was religious in nature. Ten or twelve preachers would arrive and they preached around the clock, day and night for about two weeks. This was a social occasion and people brought their picnic baskets for their breakfast, lunch and dinner. The people also listened to band concerts, sang hymns and enjoyed a swim in the crystal water of Lake Erie on the edge of the park. Then they listened to another sermon, just as they would listen to another speaker at a conference today.

Gradually, people wanted to stay longer during the hot weather and live in the tents. In time my uncle arrived with his barber shop and a hotel is built. Then hot dogs, popcorn and saltwater toffee are sold in stands. Post cards are for sale and some people prefer to stay in the hotel rather than a tent. Your children could enjoy a ride on a merry-go-round or a little boat or canoe. Soon the concessions grew to the point where no one preached anymore and the amusement park evolved as did a complete Village of Crystal Beach.

Rebstock's farm was the central part of Crystal Beach. The Haune and Bradville farms were developed as well and building-lots were sold off to people like my mother and father in 1917. They bought on Alexandra road and built the first house there. We have pictures of a dirt road, a path on the side of the road and then a wooden sidewalk.

When Aunt Jenny first came here she bought a building-lot and built a one room little shed with a hand water pump in the front yard for fresh water and an outhouse in the back yard. She rented her shed for the summer. Gradually she added a bedroom, a bathroom and continued to rent during the summer until she bought the lot next door. In this way she expanded her real estate ownership. From 1917 until 1930 there was a population boom in Crystal Beach. And everyone went to the beach in the afternoon. No one stayed in their hot homes or cottages.

In the winter in the days before electrical refrigeration, my dad used to go out onto the Lake Erie ice near The Buffalo Canoe Club and cut ice for the Teal brothers. They had this huge ice storage house with sawdust insulation and they sold ice door to door in the summer. I worked on the ice-truck in the summer as a kid and we delivered these 25 and 50 pound pieces of ice. We'd put the ice into the iceboxes in the back part of their kitchens. With one hundred thousand people living along the lake from Fort Erie to Crystal Beach, you can see where the Teals had a fantastic business. Electric refrigeration didn't come along until the 1940's. During the winter, the Teals sold people coal to keep them warm.

But in the summer the people had ice for their Canadian beer and highballs, their eggs, milk, cream, butter and even ice cream. The iceman delivered your ice to your door, a vegetable truck delivered veggies, a bakery man delivered your bread, a milkman delivered your milk, eggs, butter etc. Many farmers had their own door to door egg run. Most people went to the

Aunt Jenny, age 19, 1914.
Harvey Holzworth Collection

butcher shop for their meat. Our member of parliament, Girve Fretz and his brother, used to deliver their mother's home-made pies door to door. During the depression, everyone was trying to make a buck.

Honey Teal had an interesting job. He and his father used to run the honey wagon. Aunt Jenny loved everyone including Honey Teal and everyone loved her. Every Christmas Honey Teal brought Jenny a jar of prune juice. That was their joke. In return, Aunt Jenny brought Honey a dozen oranges and a dozen bananas. The Teal boys were all husky people who worked the ice truck, the coal truck and they also worked the honey wagon. One day Aunt Jenny was renting a cottage to some girls and Aunt Jenny shouted, "Hello there Honey." And Honey replied, "Hello there Jenny, how are you?" The girls were surprised to hear this and said, "You called him Honey. Is he your boyfriend?" And Jenny explained that Honey ran the honey wagon.

Everyone had outdoor toilets with tin cans that received their human waste when the toilet was used. Twice a week, someone had to lift those pails of human waste out of the outdoor toilets and place them at the curb, much like garbage cans. Then two nights a week, Honey had the sweet smelling job of dumping those pails of human waste into his honey wagon and then dumping a wagon full of human urine and feces at his farm. This job disappeared in 1927 when Crystal Beach put in underground sewers and paved the streets. This was one of the first sewer systems in southern Ontario.

My father and his brothers were very handy as painters, electricians and builders. When my uncle wanted to expand his hotel, he'd call the family and together they would build whatever was needed. The central part of the building was like any store in any downtown section but they gradually built on top and sideways. It was always in a state of flux.

My uncle Ed closed the hotel in 1964. He was in the process of building the first cocktail lounge in Crystal Beach. For such a lounge you had to have carpeting, chesterfields to sit on, indirect lighting and proper cocktail tables. You couldn't just have chairs, tables and a linoleum floor. He already had the contract and the drawings and was about to convert the front ladies beverage room into a cocktail lounge.

53

Suddenly, my aunt developed a severe form of cancer and she could not function in the hotel. We had a family meeting and discussed what should happen. They owned three houses over by the roller coaster on Erie Road. Everyone said that they should sell the hotel and move into a house. At that point his beer license was only the second license in Crystal Beach and such a license was worth a fortune. They had marvellous offers for the hotel but as uncle Ed said, "This has been our home all our lives and we've lived here for 60 years as a married couple. Why should we move away?" So they just closed the barroom. That was tough on Aunt Ida and Aunt Jenny because they didn't have a job in the barroom anymore. But they didn't have to work as hard and they were glad for the quiet. But they were busy because they had their 13 houses to run as well as the hotel without the barroom. Jenny took boarders until 1969 when she closed the dining room and then only roomers. Aunt Abby died at 71 years of age of her cancer. Aunt Jenny nursed my Uncle Ed until he was 94.

When it got too much for Aunt Jenny she asked me to move her over to this house. It was built by my father and Uncle Jim for Aunt Jenny as her home. That's why it is not as cottagey. She never knew when she would have to move out of the hotel. Plus, she came close to getting married three times and this was to be their house. But until she was 81 she never got to live here.

Back to their hotel history. They had a dining room. Then they were allowed to sell beer. Their first beer was called four/four beer which was much like water. One year later the Americans under Franklin Delano Roosevelt could drink three/two beer which was weaker yet. So with all the American patrons, there were lines formed to get into the dining room to drink beer with their meals.

Then they received the first license in the whole Niagara district to serve full strength Canadian beer around 1934 and the line formed down the street all spring, summer and fall. The Queen's Hotel in Ridgeway got theirs about a week later and of course Niagara Falls and Fort Erie came about a month later.

With the arrival of the good beer, it was bedlam. I was about eight years old. The people were lined down the street and around the block. Patrons were limited to four beers and then they had to leave by the exit door to allow more people to enter.

It's interesting that up until that time there were no legal public outlets in Ontario, Canada where you could go and drink alcohol. You could buy alcohol in the liquor store but you had to take it home to drink it. As far as beer was concerned, most people did not drink bottled beer. When it became available in the hotel, the kegs of draft beer were electrically refrigerated in the cellar and there were taps. Ice kept things cool in the home but in the bar, beer was kept cool electrically and was it ever good in the hot summers and did they ever sell it!

Historically there were a lot of things that happened here. The first general store, the first post office, the first treasurer and justice of the peace, the first court and the first full strength Canadian beer.

Aunt Ida applied for the position of post mistress, probably through Alf Wilson our Member of Parliament. Since she was staying at the hotel, this job gave her a little income. Then a post office was built at the Circle and George Rebstock was given the postmaster's job. That meant that Aunt Ida and George Rebstock didn't speak to each other for about a year. Aunt Ida was hurt that without any warning, the new postmaster was George Rebstock until he retired.

After we had the men boarding at the hotel who built the Crystal Ball Room, we had the workers who were working on the new Welland Canal. The work project lasted about nine years. Workers were imported from all over the world. Port Colborne and Welland didn't have enough room for them so fifty boarders were brought to the hotel. They had breakfast before work in the morning, a packed lunch and then fifty men for dinner at night. Two buses would bring them back and forth. Can you imagine the work for these four people? My Uncle Ed did the roasts and turkeys, my aunts baked the bread and pies and made the potatoes and then my Aunts Ida and Jenny served the tables. There were only eighteen rooms in the hotel so the boarders must have been packed with three to a room.

The Faiazza brothers were cement and stone masons who came from Italy to work on the canal and boarded here. They liked Crystal Beach so much that when the canal was finished they bought a little house here and opened a business, The Faiazza Brothers Cement Works. If you look at all the older sidewalks of Crystal Beach, there's a little imprint on the corner that says, "Faiazza Brothers Contractors Crystal Beach." They built every sidewalk in the Village of Crystal Beach and did very well elsewhere.

Bart Faiazza's daughter, Madeline was the mayor of Fort Erie. She went to Ridgeway High School and was very bright. With regional government, she was elected Fort Erie's representative. Her mother, Mrs. Faiazza had seven girls and one boy and she often visited with Aunt Jenny. Their birthdays coincided so that they celebrated together.

My mother's very best friend was a Mrs. Butler. She and her husband owned the miniature railway in Crystal Beach in the early days when it was a Chautauqua, long before incorporation as a village. During the winter they used to travel to Crystal Beach Florida, also founded by J.E. Rebstock. The two families traveled in their own mobile homes. The Butlers had an old bus remodelled into a house. In 1925 the trip to Florida would take about ten days. There they would spend the winter and then return to Crystal Beach, Canada in the spring.

For three years as a young boy, I used to deliver the Toronto Star to the home of J.E. Rebstock, the founder of Crystal Beach. At that point he had a very pretty second wife who was much younger and who used to be his nurse. She was a kind and lovely lady who used to say, "Come in and have a glass of milk and a cookie," on a cold winter's night when I delivered her paper.

Then I would see the 94 year-old gentleman sitting by the fireplace with his robe over him. I have always felt privileged that I knew the man who founded Crystal Beach.

"They screamed pretty loudly."
Mimi Fischer

When my boyfriend and I were 12 years old, we snuck between the Tunnel of Love and the game where one picks a floating toy from a running little stream. When we were in that small space, we would open the service door for the Tunnel of Love and step into the display with the dummies. Then we would pose with the scenery. When the boats came by we would jump at them and scare the boaters. They screamed pretty loudly. It was fun for them and for us as well.

Did anyone tell you how the poor kids got in the park after they started to charge admission? They had their rich friend go into the park, pay to get his hand stamped and then run out of the park. He then placed the back of his hand on the back of the hand of his friend to transfer the Crystal Beach stamp. What little devils! But I'm sure that God forgave them.

" The nuns organized an outing for the first communion class."
Joseph Buckley

I recall the first time that I went to Crystal Beach. I was a fourth grader at Saint Casimir School on Buffalo's East side. The nuns organized an outing for the first communion class. It was a Canadiana ferry ride from the foot of Main Street to a day at Crystal Beach.

The nuns had our parental permission and we hopped a Clinton Street streetcar toward downtown. This was the spring of 1940 and the weather

Aerial View of Crystal Beach Park, July 5, 1978.
Courtesy of Buffalo State College, Courier Collection

Crystal Beach Boat at dock and Comet coaster.
Courtesy of Buffalo State College, Courier Collection

was pleasant. At the end of the street car route we walked through Shelton Square and then down Main Street toward the ferry dock where the Canadiana was waiting.

The dock was crowded as we boarded. From the highest deck we watched as the Canadiana pulled away from the dock. It was exciting to see the water and to get a view of the city and crowds. And I liked the loud music as well. We were free to walk around the boat. That was the first time that I saw an engine-room with a huge steam pump propelling the boat. After an hour we got a view of Crystal Beach and heard the screams from the people on the roller coasters.

The nuns allowed us to walk around unsupervised in the Park as well but with orders to behave and stay near. With limited funds we were still able to go on some rides, eat and admire the interesting rides. Food booths, a huge dance hall, a large assortment of fairway rides was more then enough to take up our day. I returned many times as I was growing up. Even as a young adult I returned on a date or in groups to dance and enjoy the fairway.

John E. Rebstock Obituary
Buffalo Evening News, March 21, 1941

J. E. REBSTOCK

John E. Rebstock died in his 89th year. Death came in Douglas Memorial Hospital, Fort Erie after he sacrificed his second leg in a vain attempt to hold onto life. One leg was amputated last September to stop the spread of a gangrenous infection.

He was born in Black Rock, New York of parents who had emigrated from Germany with the Schoellkopfs. He developed Tonawanda Street and the Riverside Park area.

In 1889, he became interested in the sandy stretches along Lake Erie's Canadian shore, desolate from Fort Erie all the way to Port Colborne. Mr. Rebstock chose a hundred-acre stretch from the Humberstone Road to the lake. Its east and west boundaries are now Ridge and Oxford Roads, thus embracing almost all of the present resort cottage lands as well as the whole amusement and bathing area.

Bren Gun Girl Ronnie Foster in 1941, when nylons came in two pieces.
She assembled machine guns for World War II during the day
and danced the jitterbug at night.
Library and Archives Canada

Buffalo needed a bathing spot, so he and his associates charted a boat to carry passengers from the foot of Main Street and improvised a dock here. There were few amusements.

As the popularity of the beach grew, Mr. Rebstock decided to lay it out as a camp meeting ground. He never dreamed that one day motorists would find its lanes narrow or cumbersome.

Ironically, it was the automobile, which hurt Crystal Beach, with the building of the Peace Bridge, Buffalo folk found a variety of bathing spots along the shore. Theretofore, they had come almost entirely by boat and then only to this beach.

Sold Out to C. & B.

In 1906, a typhoid attack laid Mr. Rebstock low, so he and his associates accepted the offer of the Cleveland & Buffalo Transit Company interests for the beach. Mr. Rebstock retained a stock interest and kept title to most of the land for development purposes. When his health returned, he bought further lands to extend Crystal Beach west to Schooley Road, then added Bay Beach. Mr. Rebstock leaves his second wife, Mamie, two sons, Postmaster George J. who assisted him in the real estate business and Walter J., builder here; two daughters, Mrs. Robert Teal of Fort Erie North and Miss Thelma, librarian in Bangor, Maine, 12 grandchildren and two great-grandchildren.

Funeral services will be held Sunday afternoon in Dell's Funeral Home, Ridgeway, the Rev. C.L. Poole of the United Church officiating. Mr. Rebstock was a Mason.

"At night under a full moon, the lovers could..."
Thomas M. Rizzo

I spent five summers as a musician on the S.S. Canadiana, also known as the Crystal Beach Boat. That was in 1943 and from 1946 through 1949. The band played seven days a week, Monday through Saturday from 8 p.m. until 1 a.m. and on Sunday from 2 p.m. until 11 p.m. For me it wasn't work. It was fun.

The boat was a turn of the century steamship built in Buffalo and was launched March 5, 1910. It was to accommodate 2500 passengers and a crew of 34. It was said to have carried over 15 million passengers in the 46 years it sailed across Lake Erie. Service terminated at the end of the 1956 season because of an interracial riot that occurred on board on Memorial Day, 1956. This incident marred the previously peaceful and accident free career of the ship and signaled the drastic decline in patronage.

That's a brief history of the boat. But what was the magic? What was the attraction for this grand lady?

A good part of it was getting to the boat. I'm sure that you remember that in the nineteen forties, automobiles were not widely available. In fact, the parking lot alongside the boat-dock could only accommodate about 100 cars. Considering that the boat could accommodate 2500 passengers, it follows that most people took public transportation to get to it. The IRC buses, forerunner of the NFTA, took you to Shelton Square, which for young people was a reasonable walking distance to the boat dock. However, the elderly and the not so athletic transferred to a trolley. The streetcar dropped them at lower Main Street and then it was a very short walk to the dock at the foot of Commercial Street. But before you got to the dock, you had to maneuver past the popcorn, peanut and balloon vendors.

History tells us that the first settlements in any city are located near water. Buffalo was no exception and one of the first streets was Dante Place, which led to the dock. Here there was a proliferation of saloons and brothels which catered to the seafarers. Many of these same buildings were still standing and were occupied in the 1940's. But the saloons and brothels were now living quarters for the poorest of immigrants, mostly Italian. But the crowd of people rushing to the boat and to Crystal Beach hardly took notice of the plight of the poor people who lived there. It's interesting to note that this poorest of neighborhoods has become the choicest of waterfront property.

Long before it was called marketing, the management of The Crystal Beach Transit Co. showed great skill in promoting the boat and Crystal Beach. There were special days for specific neighborhoods such as Kensington-Bailey Day, Riverside Day, West Side Day, and Kenmore Day etc. Booths were set up in the main intersection of the neighborhood so that you could pre-purchase your boat and amusement tickets at a discount. The Buffalo Evening News had a special coupon for additional discounts. I remember the brightly painted booth at the corner of Grant and Ferry Streets. A great deal of money poured into these booths and I don't recall seeing an armed guard standing near one, neither here at the dock or at Crystal Beach. It was truly a different time. And when your special day finally arrived, you felt that you were going on an all day outing with your friends and neighbors.

If you didn't pre-purchase your boat ticket, you had to do so at an outdoor ticket booth at the dock. The regular price in the early forties was 75 cents for adults and 25 cents for children. After your purchase you were herded into a dark-damp enclosure to await boarding. Finally the cyclone fence gate opened and the momentum of the crowd carried you on board the boat over a six-foot wide gangplank. This boat was so large that you needed to prearrange a meeting place in case you got separated from your friends or family.

There were three passenger decks on this elegant boat. The first deck had the gangplank that you crossed to board. It also had a cocktail lounge that was not as fancy as that sounds. There was a bar where you could buy great Canadian ale. Plus a hotdog stand where the hot dogs sold so quickly that the vendors barely had time to warm them up before serving them.

There were also two or three Claw Machines where you could try your luck to grab a prize, a prize that seemed cemented to the bottom of the case.

Plus, there was a whole row of five-cent slot machines that we called one-armed bandits. You could not play these while the boat was docked but as soon as the boat cleared the breakwall there was a mad dash to try your luck. The same prohibition against playing the slots was true as you approached the Canadian shore. I always wondered why the lake was considered international waters for gambling purposes when half the lake belonged to the United States and the other half belonged to Canada. Kids were not supposed to play these machines and the crew was constantly shooing the kids away. But it was a terrible temptation. I suspect that some of the kids didn't get to ride the Cyclone at Crystal Beach because too many nickels went into the slot machines. When I returned from military service in 1946 the slots were gone. It was probably an anti-gambling group that got them removed.

Also from the first deck you could lean over a metal barrier and look down into the bowels of the ship. You could actually look into the engine room, smell the oily engines and feel the rhythmic throb as the ship plied its way through the water.

The inside stairway to the second deck was truly Victorian. There was a brass chandelier suspended over the staircase. The staircase was made of rich mahogany. The inside cabin of the second deck was also mahogany and was enclosed with leaded glass windows. At the top of the stairs, strategically placed was the mirrored, mahogany ice cream and candy stand that featured Rich's Ice Cream.

You could go fore or aft from this inside cabin. If you went fore, you were outside at the front of the boat where you could sit for the entire ride. If you went aft, you crossed the enormous, highly polished dance floor that had a raised bandstand at one end and a Wurlitzer jukebox at the other. On the bandstand sat an old upright piano. A piano is basically a stringed instrument that suffers from the elements. With high humidity, temperature changes and little kids banging on it when there was no supervision, it was impossible to keep the piano in tune.

On either side of the dance floor, next to the outer railings, were park benches. Here the passengers could sit and listen to the music and watch the dancers. On windy or cold nights the crew would roll down the side curtains. The boat always creaked and groaned as it made its way across the lake but this was especially unnerving on nights when the lake was rough. One of the more famous musicians to play on that bandstand was Harold Arlen. I often wondered if the inspiration for his song, Stormy Weather, came from his experiences on the Crystal Beach Boat.

The third deck was the favorite of kids in the daytime and lovers at night. It too was lined with park benches. During the day, the youngsters could romp at will. At night, with the only light coming from the moon, the lovers could…well you know. Also on the third deck you could see the 6 lifeboats and the hundreds of life jackets. I don't think that anyone ever gave them more than a passing glance.

Above the third deck, was the wheelhouse where the Captain directed the voyage. He had a great toy up there. The Whistle. He tooted it when he left Buffalo harbor and when he approached the Canadian shore and the same on the return trip. He also tooted it when he passed other boats on the lake. That blast was deafening if you were on the third deck.

It took only 45 minutes to travel the 12 miles across Lake Erie to Crystal Beach. But you could pack a lot of dancing, romancing and fun into that short time. There were as many as 6 round trips per day beginning at 10 a.m. from Buffalo and ending at 11:45 p.m. from Crystal Beach. This last boat arrived in Buffalo close to 1 a.m.

The trip that was the most fun for me during the week was the 8 p.m. crossing to the Beach. The boat was loaded with teenagers and young adults who were revved up for an exciting evening. Just as much fun was the 11:45 p.m. return trip when that same group was still wound up about the night's activities. The music that we played going over to Crystal Beach was jazzy while coming back the music was dreamy.

But playing on the boat was quite different from playing in a ballroom. There was always some movement of the boat. This meant that if you played an instrument like a bass fiddle, you had to keep your balance. Like the piano, many instruments were affected by humidity. So playing in tune with the band was another challenge. There were humid nights when I thought that my bass fiddle strings were rubber bands. Electrified instruments were another horror story. Those instruments were designed to be powered by a steady alternating current. But the boat generated its direct current. And just as the illumination from lamps would change depending on the variation in the direct current, so too would the sound vary coming out of our electric organs, vibraphones and guitars. This was such a problem that we finally gave up using them.

Despite the problems, we had a lot of fun. So too did the dancers who danced beneath the steel crossbeam that carried an order, "NO JEEPING." I'll bet that no one under the age of 75 has any idea what that meant. Jeeping was a dance craze in the late 1930's. It was a rhythmic hop. It was forbidden on the boat because it was thought that too many people dancing the JEEP in synch could somehow cause the boat to tip. This information was important to a friend of mine who recently told me how relieved she was to finally find out. It seems that she had gone to a very fine Catholic high school for girls where the secret word was that Jeeping was on the same level as one of the seven deadly sins.

But don't think for a moment that the band had nothing to do between the 9 p.m. arrival at Crystal Beach and the 11:45 p.m. departure back to Buffalo. Before the boat docked at Crystal, we gathered up all of our instruments, including my base fiddle. Then the band was the first to leave the boat and we literally ran along the dock, through Canadian Customs to the Crystal Beach Ballroom. If we had not run, we would have been trampled by the stampede of passengers behind us, all eager to get to the park.

In the ballroom, we relieved the Canadian band such as Bert Niosi or Maynard Ferguson from Toronto. They needed a break because the music was continuous. It was called Park Plan Dancing where dancers paid 10 cents a dance. There was no charge to enter the ballroom, only a charge if you wanted to dance. That's why the management did not want any lulls in the music.

The ballroom was a beautiful structure with a cantilevered wide expanse on the dance floor, without any supporting floor posts or pillars. That floor could accommodate 1500 couples. The revolving mirrored ball on the ceiling appeared to be crystal and reflected sparkling dots of light from several colored spotlights. Around the perimeter of the dance floor were tables and chairs for spectators who could also enjoy the music.

In addition to the Park Plan Dancing there were special events at the Ballroom that charged an admission fee. It was the era of the big bands and they all played there: Tommy Dorsey, Jimmy Dorsey, Les Brown, Gene Krupa, Louie Prima, to name a few. It was one of the premiere ballrooms in North America and these bands played to sellout audiences. The sound system was exceptional. Of course, it had to be considering it had to overcome the noise from the Cyclone rollercoaster and other nearby rides.

At 11:30 p.m. we heard the Canadiana Captain toot his warning whistle. The boat did not wait for anyone. If you didn't make the last trip of the night then you were stranded. At the warning whistle we packed our instruments and made the reverse dash from ballroom to boat. That was six nights a week. Fortunately, I was in better shape then than I am today.

But Sunday was something else. The Park was closed because of Canadian Blue laws. But the Canadiana was used for a cruise on Lake Erie. Sunday afternoon was reserved for Canadians. The empty boat left Buffalo harbor at 1 p.m. It picked up Canadian passengers at 2 p.m. and cruised the lake for 3 hours until 5 p.m. This was a quiet group of mostly older people, the 40 to 50 year old crowd who I considered old at that time. Five hundred passengers were considered a good crowd. In an attempt to increase the turnout, Harold Austin introduced floorshows on the afternoon cruise in 1943. We had dancers, singers, magicians etc. It didn't help. It was a quiet crowd that wanted a quiet afternoon boat ride.

The boat then traveled to Buffalo empty, arriving at 6 p.m. and readied itself for the 8 p.m. three hour MOONLIGHT CRUISE.

If the weather was nice it was normal to have over 2000 passengers on the Sunday night cruise. We had a ten-piece orchestra that could play as loudly as it liked because there were no neighbors to complain. Harold Austin was a great promoter who had jobs for the best musicians on the boat and at the Dellwood Ballroom. The music was great. The crowd was responsive.

Labor Day was closing day at Crystal Beach. All the hype and hoopla of the season culminated at 11:45 p.m. as the boat left the Canadian shore. Fireworks filled the sky. The band on the boat played Auld Lang Syne.

It was fun. I have fond memories of the boat and ballroom. I am delighted to have been part of that Crystal Beach experience.

"... the kids would pester me for a ride."

Lorne McKenney

I got interested in Crystal Beach because of my neighbour, Louie Lejeune, who owned a gravel pit next to our farm. I worked at the washer at the gravel pit when Louie was washing gravel. He asked me to go to Crystal Beach in 1945 and 1946 to help on the train ride and auto ride and to help clean up the Park. We had to change railroad ties on the miniature railroad. Plus, I would sit on the cow-catcher on the front of the engine and oil the track as the train made its circuit. This was part of the maintenance.

Louie owned the train and the auto ride. He also had the parking lot by the round house where the railroad was located and another parking lot on the street.

Lorne McKenny proudly displays a wheel from the miniature railway train.
Photo by ERNO ROSSI

Louie had a bull's penis preserved by a taxidermist and Louie displayed his trophy on his office wall. Women would come into his office and ask about the wall display. Louie would hand the trophy to the women and asked them to sniff it and guess what it was. They were always red-faced when he finally told them the truth.

When I was running the auto ride, the kids would come up to me and pester me for a free ride. I couldn't give them a ride. Instead, I'd tell them to go to the machine shop and fetch me a track-jack. They would try several times, but always got the same answer. That's when I had to tell them, "No track-jack-no free ride."

"We were bad buggers!"

Ray Andrews

We used to hang out at Crystal Beach when we were kids. My brother worked at one of the booths and I visited him quite often. We would sneak through the fence at the Cyclone roller coaster and pick up nickels and dimes that fell from above.

I remember seeing Tommy and Jimmy Dorsey in the late forties. Glenn Miller was there. So was Tex Beneke who took over Glenn Miller's band. Duke Ellington came as well as part of the summer circuit.

We would drive to Buffalo and leave our car. We would then go to the liquor store and buy all this strange booze—a mickey of this and a mickey of that and we would take this on to the Canadiana for the ride to Crystal Beach. We would get hammered at the bar and with our own booze. When we got off the boat at Crystal Beach we would hop the bus for the ride back to Buffalo to pick up our car. One time I left a mickey of booze in the toilet tank on the Canadiana as we left the ship. The next week we came back and that bottle was still there! We were bad buggers. We'd get hammered on that boat and then leave.

"...played marbles with goat droppings."

Harold Austin's Pet Show

Between 1935 and 1955 musician Harold Austin performed with his band in the Crystal Ballroom. During the 1930's Austin played for large crowds during dance marathons and for the Miss New York Beauty Pageants. One of Austin's acts was to bring his dog Spot to the dance floor. Spot would stand on his hind legs and howl to the tune of, My Country Tis of Thee.

The Hall brothers used a Great Dane dog and two live lambs as part of their act on the ballroom floor. Harold Austin however was prepared in the event of an accident by the dog or lambs. Yes, there was an accident. One lamb deposited on the dance floor a mound of brown, round droppings much to the delight of the thousands of spectators. Austin sent in Cliff, the sax player to save the day.

Cliff put on a lady's hat and pretended to spank the lamb. He then created a circle on the dance floor with a large piece of string. Cliff then got down on his knees and played marbles with lamb droppings. The thunderous laughter from the thousands of spectators was the longest and loudest in Crystal Ballroom history.

"... these were indeed Happy Days."

Marian Basty

One of my favorite memories of Crystal Beach and its boat is the Catholic Youth Organization Day. It consisted of teenagers from various Buffalo/WNY parishes. We sailed on the Crystal Beach Boat to the Crystal Beach pier with joyous yelling but no riots.

Then with handfuls of ride tickets we headed for the midway. Only brave people like my sister Barb would ride the Comet coaster with its high point next to Lake Erie.

Most of us brought swimsuits and headed for the beautiful sand beach. The boys always splashed big waves of water on the girls who gingerly entered the water one toe at a time. Our wonderful pastor actually showed up in his swim trunks! Heavens! We never thought of him as a beach guy. I was a teenager in 1945-50 and these were indeed Happy Days.

"... draped pants that were tight at the cuff..."

Barbara Basty Fernandez

My husband remembers an incident regarding the Canadiana. At the time, draped pants that were tight at the cuff and very full at the knee were not allowed on the boat. He and his friends were waiting in line to get on the boat and they spotted a fellow up on the boat-deck wearing a white suit with draped pants. He was waving to someone in line. My husband could never figure out how he got on board with those draped pants.

"My first real job at 13 years of age was to run the mail down to the Canadiana."

Paul Kassay, Mr. Crystal Beach

During the early 1940's my parents visited booming Crystal Beach and decided to move there from Welland. As a child I was enrolled in Ridgeway Public School and lived on Oxford Street in a tourist home. Because many visitors missed the last boat back to Buffalo, they would stay overnight in our tourist home. On many nights two siblings and I were bumped out of bed to the attic and our room was given to people who took the first boat in the morning back to Buffalo. Even our attic was shared by strangers when the house was full. My mother would use sheets suspended

Paul Kassay and his Crystal Beach Ballroom microphone.
Photo by ERNO ROSSI

into partitions to shield the strangers from her kids and the strangers were very grateful for the overnight shelter. My mom even used a lawn swing with a sheet over it to create an overnight tent for patrons.

In time my parents bought cottages and during the six week summer we worked like crazy to keep up with the demand. But my parents spent the winters in Miami.

My first real job at about 13 years of age was to run the mail down to the Canadiana at the dock and receive the Buffalo mail from the Purser and bring it to the post office.

As kids we did not have much money. Consequently we begged for unused Crystal Beach Park tickets from people who were leaving the Park. The Hall brothers didn't like us begging for tickets because unused Park tickets meant more money in their pockets. That's why they booted us out of the Park when they caught us.

We would swim near the dock on the beach-side when people were lined up to board or leave the Canadiana. These people would throw coins to us in the water and we would dive for them. I'm sure there are many coins that we missed still buried in the sand.

We were happy as well when the Park was closed after Labor Day because we had the free run of the dock and beach for swimming. But soon the weather cooled and fall and winter were upon us.

I remember the celebration by Americans and Canadians in the Queen's Circle when World War Two ended in 1945. The place went crazy.

During the winter our parents enrolled us in school in Miami. That's where I met my future wife who eventually moved to Crystal Beach.

I'd watch the candy-kiss maker, George Horne, lift these huge pots of boiling liquid sugar. He'd dump the mixture onto the cooling table and then run it through a machine.

When George made the suckers they went along the conveyor belt where there was a cooling duct to harden them. Often you'd have to pick out the bees during the late summer because they got right into the machine. But I never ate a bee. I'd wrap kisses, make popcorn, roast peanuts and package suckers. In the afternoon, I'd restock the concession stands as they ran low on these treats.

As an assistant candy maker at Halls Suckers for the summer of 1956, I earned about 35 dollars a week. That was the life style here at the time. Work the summer and go on pogey (unemployment insurance) for the winter. Spring was especially welcomed because the unemployment payments had run out.

In time I opened my own photo studio and gathered news clips for newspapers and TV. If you watched Channel 7 in Buffalo you have probably seen film that I have shot. This lasted for 25 years.

Along the way, a Buffalo News reporter gave me the title of Mr. Crystal Beach. After the Park closed, Bob Long and I, along with Cathy Herbert, Rick Doan and several other people decided to create Crystal Beach Memory Days. We kept the memory of Crystal Beach alive. Plus Cathy, myself and Janet Truckenbrodt produced a video, The Life And Times Of Crystal Beach that still sells today.

We enjoyed the ride on the Canadiana and the American beer to the extent that we would ride that boat back and forth to Buffalo at least three times in one day. Once I was having such a good time partying when I got to Buffalo that I missed the last boat home. That's when I knew that I had a friend when I called him to drive to Buffalo and pick me up because I had missed the boat.

Why did the Canadiana stop running? Several reasons come to mind. The riot that occurred there on Memorial Day 1956 was a nail in the coffin. There were union problems, the boat needed maintenance, it wasn't paying and it wasn't up to Coastguard Standards. Cars were plentiful and competed with the Crystal Beach Boat. Instead of it bringing thousands of people each day by boat, people had to come by car or bus. There were lineups of vehicles for miles all the way to Number 3 Highway. That, combined with charging admission to the Park in place of free admission, added to the decline of the Park. Competition from other amusement parks also added to the decline.

I remember going to the Crystal Ballroom. Johnnie Ray, Vaughn Monroe, Stan Kenton, Bert Niosi, Guy Lombardo, Glenn Miller, Jimmy Dorsey, thousands of people on that dance floor. What a shame that the dancehall was torn down to be replaced by cookie cutter cottages. From the dancehall I saved hand painted posters of the entertainers. One is autographed by Tex Beneke. Plus I've got the two old fashioned microphones used by the vocalists who appeared there. How sad that you don't know what you've got until it's gone.

Engineer Roy Taylor and Marie Burkot are ready for a run on a new edition of an 1863 locomotive.
Courtesy of Buffalo State College, Courier Collection

Ed and Filmore Hall.
Cathy Herbert Collection

George C. Hall
President

Edward G. Hall
Vice President

George C. Hall, Jr.
Treasurer

F. L. Hall
Secretary and
General Manager

Crystal Beach Transit CO., INC.
Foot of Commercial Street,
Buffalo 2, New York
PHONE: WA. 3585-6

STEAMER Canadiana
Capacity 2500 Passengers

March 23, 1956

Dear Sir:

We are now booking our group picnics for 1956 and believe it would be to your advantage if some serious thought would be given to having a picnic this year at BEAUTIFUL CRYSTAL BEACH.

Many other groups have their picnics annually at Crystal Beach and find we have an IDEAL SPOT FOR AN IDEAL DAY OF FUN AND FROLIC. If your group be large or small, we are in a position to offer you A PERFECT PICNIC PLAN THAT CAN NOT BE DUPLICATED ANYWHERE.

I would like to suggest, it would be to your advantage to bring this matter before your group at an early date, with the thought in mind that you are then in a position to get a picnic date of your choice by booking early.

Attached you will find a list of pertinent information for a picnic at Crystal Beach.

The writer will be most happy to meet you or your representatives at any time to further discuss in detail a picnic plan.

Looking forward to an early reply and a personal meeting, I remain,

Cordially yours,
CRYSTAL BEACH TRANSIT COMPANY
George A. Schmied, Gen. Passenger Agent
GAS: Jhr
Enc.

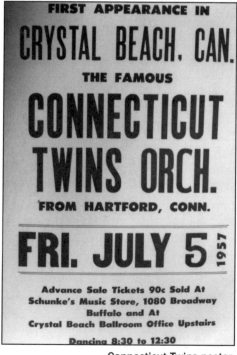

Connecticut Twins poster.
Photo by ERNO ROSSI - Cathy Herbert Collection

We are listing some of the details, advantages and facilities available for a plant or group picnic at BEAUTIFUL CRYSTAL BEACH.

1. CRYSTAL BEACH is an ideal spot for a plant or group picnic with its glorious setting of natural beauty with flower gardens in bloom all summer long, tree shaded picnic grove, unsurpassed bathing beach and an exciting million dollar midway, without dust (the entire park has been blacktopped, eliminating all dust and gravel.)

2. In the Park proper are over 70 major rides and amusements, including a modern KIDDIE LAND with 12 SAFE MINIATURE RIDES for the small fry. Many new, unique rides have been added during the past few years and I assure you there is excitement, thrills and a day of fun for every employee and his family.

3. The natural bathing beach is one of the FINEST, SAFEST and CLEANEST inland bathing beaches on the continent. A modern aerated bath house provides a clean comfortable place for changing and a safe deposit for checking valuables. A trained corps of life guards are constantly on the alert, assuring full protection of the bathers at all times.

4. Our beautiful tree shaded picnic grove has a comfortable seating capacity exceeding 6000 and is located immediately adjacent to the large restaurant and cafeteria, where coffee, milk and other additional needs can be obtained and added to the family picnic basket or complete meals ordered by those not wishing to carry their own food.

5. Two modern athletic fields, with one-Quarter mile cinder tracks and two large stadiums, both equipped with P.A. systems are provided free for your games and athletic events. Experienced attendants with many years of picnic supervision will be available to help your game committee. A modern FIRST AID STATION is located in the athletic field proper for emergency purposes.

6. Our lovely Stardust Ballroom offers real pleasure for those who enjoy the best in dancing.

7. If the management or union desires to contribute financially towards free food or drinks, this can be easily arranged through special food and refreshment tickets supplied by us, which can be desired, but you are only billed for the tickets used.

8. We will also allow you a 33-1/3% discount on all amusement tickets, which come in strips of ten. Although the regular cost is 60¢ per strip,

your cost will be only 40¢ per strip of ten. It is not necessary to order any set number as you are only billed for the ones actually used.

9. Everyone will enjoy the delightful, one hour boat ride on our all-steel modern Steamer "Canadiana", which is very relaxing and invigorating. We will also allow you a fifty-percent discount on the regular fare (adults and children) on this happy, 25 mile round trip boat ride. Plenty of parking space is available at our Buffalo Terminal and also in the Park proper for those who wish to drive.

10. Appropriate posters will be provided publicizing the picnic so that they may be placed in advantageous spots throughout your plant or area.

11. The above plus numerous other facilities found only at BEAUTIFUL CRYSTAL BEACH assures EVERYONE attending the picnic (Wives, Kiddies, Sweethearts) a grand and glorious time.

12. The writer will be very glad to attend a Board or Committee meeting and further explain in detail what we have to offer and answer any questions which may arise, and show you why the largest industrial plants and groups in this area have their picnics EVERY YEAR AT BEAUTIFUL CRYSTAL BEACH.

Cordially Yours for a Happy Picnic
CRYSTAL BEACH TRANSIT COMPANY

George A. Schmied, Gen. Passenger Agent

Canadiana arrives at Crystal Beach on her maiden voyage from Buffalo on May 30, 1910.
Courtesy Buffalo State College, Courier Collection

The Canadiana

By Michael Vogel
Courtesy, W.N.Y Heritage Institute

She was once the princess of the lakes, the stuff of childhood dreams and moonlit romances.

For generations of Buffalonians, the Canadiana meant a sundappled voyage bright with anticipation and hours later, a homeward cruise under starry summer skies to the music of a shipboard orchestra.

The Canadiana and her slightly older sister, the Americana, were the Crystal Beach Boats—the ships that took young and old on a 75 minute journey from Buffalo to Crystal Beach Amusement Park on the shore near Point Abino, Ontario. For those who knew the vessels, their names will always be mixed with the magic of youth and summer.

The Americana debuted in 1908, designed by eminent naval architect Frank E. Kirby as the first vessel of the Lake Erie Excursion Company. As the successor to a line of chartered Crystal Beach shuttle boats that had served the park since the 1890's, she added size and grace to the trade and prompted the company to add a nearly identical design to its fleet just two years later.

The Canadiana, destined to become the longer-lived and more fondly remembered of the two, was built at the Buffalo Dry Dock Co. for a quarter of a million dollars and was launched at 3 p.m. March 5, 1910. Mrs. Edward Smith, whose husband was both a director of the line and president of the Buffalo Dry Dock Co., broke the traditional bottle of champagne against the bow.

As the new steamer hit the water, a flag bearing the name Canadiana was unfurled from her masthead and the crowds ashore cheered. Carmilla M. Boland of Roble Avenue had good reason to cheer — she had submitted the winning entry in a name-the-boat contest, her suggestion edging out the names "Brittania" and "United Shores" to earn her $10 and a season's pass to the amusement park.

The new vessel measured 216 feet long, with a beam of 56 feet, and she differed little from the Americana. Unlike the Americana, the Canadiana had a small cabin for the captain's quarters behind the wheelhouse; a similar cabin would be added to the Americana in 1920 and its dance floor was enclosed, while the Canadiana's stayed open to the lake breezes.

The 974-ton Canadiana's hull was strong Swedish steel, and the overhanging steel Main Deck and steel main trunk supported a three deck wooden superstructure. Power came from a 1,446-horsepower triple-expansion steam engine, its workings visible through an opening in the Main Deck.

An ornate wood staircase led one deck upward to a forward cabin where mahogany paneling was trimmed with carvings of Neptune. The vessel's upper decks also offered promenades, benches and a bandstand and hardwood dance floor. More than a thousand lights added to the magic of the great white vessel.

The Canadiana's sea trials were held in May 1910, and her maiden voyage to Crystal Beach came on May 30. Licensed to carry 3500 passengers, she had nearly that many guests of the Lake Erie Excursion Co. aboard as she left the foot of Main Street and headed lakeward to the music of the new march, "Canadiana" by Irving Tallis.

The great white excursion steamer, belching the thick black clouds, typical of coal-burning ships of the day, drew salute after salute as she headed for open water under the command of Captain George Riley, previously captain of the Americana.

The music for the boats, in the earliest years, was furnished by the 74th Regiment Orchestra. But other musicians and their orchestras would add musical grace to the beauty of the vessel over the years — Duke Ellington. Guy Lombardo, Buffalo native and world-renowned composer Harold Arlen, Paul Whiteman, Eddie Duchin, Cab Calloway and more. Perhaps best known to those who frequently sailed on the Canadiana, was the local orchestra headed by Harold Austin.

The boat ride to Crystal Beach soon became a tradition, a magical time of summer excitement that started with the family ride on a trolley to the foot of Main Street and ended with a much more subdued trolley ride home, late at night. The day at the park, with its roller-coasters and fun houses, its all-day suckers and cotton candy, was at the heart of it all—but the hours spent on the steamboats with their powerful engines and the fascination of churning white wakes were part of the magic, too.

Summers started with the first Memorial Day voyages, and ended on Labor Day when the last steamer would pull away from the dock at Crystal Beach and pause for the season-ending fireworks display.

But there came a time when the family could drive to Crystal Beach—and that brought the beginning of the end for the great white steamers.

The Americana was the first to go, sold soon after the opening of the international Peace Bridge in 1927. She was sold to the Meseck Tug Lines in New York City, and for years ran twice-daily excursions from New York's Pier 10 to the Playland amusement park in Rye Beach, with Saturday night moonlight cruises on the Hudson River.

Later, her birth was shifted to the Battery and her destination became the Statue of Liberty until the Meseck Lines took her out of service in 1952. She was towed from Jersey City to the now-defunct Todd Shipyards in Hoboken, New Jersey, on May 11, 1953 for scrapping, and her documents were surrendered in New York that October with the note "out of documentation following change in property."

Despite rumors that she was sold for use in South America as a river steamer—rumors bolstered by the fact that Todd Shipyards did a great deal of conversion work—she probably was scrapped. She has never been re-registered under any flag, and legally no longer exists.

The Canadiana sailed on, under the Lake Erie Excursion Co. flag from 1910 to 1924, the Buffalo and Crystal Beach flag from 1924 to 1947 and the Crystal Beach Transit Co. flag from 1947 to 1956.

The line spent $30,000 to convert the Canadiana's boilers from coal-burning to oil burning in the winter of 1950-51, easing the smoke pollution but doing little to stem the loss of passenger trade to the automobile. Ticket prices were kept low to encourage the trade, but just to break even the Canadian has to sail with about 2,000 passengers—a number increasingly hard to come by.

The last straw came on Memorial Day in 1956, during what should have been the joyous opening of another summer park and sailing season.

What happened that day has been characterized as a race riot or gang rumble but probably could be described as a clash of neighborhood gangs with racial overtones. The violence of May 30, 1956 was not confined to the Canadiana—it started with a confrontation between teen gang members and three servicemen at the amusement park, and escalated into near-riot and widespread brawls.

Police from all over the Niagara Peninsula rushed to the aid of Canadian officers on duty in the small village of Crystal Beach, and an uneasy truce was imposed after nine arrests were made and the fighting died down. At 9:15 p.m., innocent park visitors and brawlers alike boarded the Canadiana for the final trip home, under the grim gaze of Canadian police.

It was a bad move. The police warnings that the trip home must be peaceful held little sway, once the steamer moved into the open lake. The Canadiana was sailing with just enough crew to get by, in the increasingly slim seasons, and there was little or no manpower for shipboard security. And to top it off, there was a gathering storm to occupy the sailors' attention.

Violence flared again, out on the lake. The trip became terrifying for parents with small children, and those who became victims of the jacketed gang members and others involved in the brawls. A Buffalo Evening News reporter described it as "a nightmare in which teenagers with ripped clothing cowered below decks while lightning split the skies outside, illuminating the marauding gangs."

Buffalo police were waiting when the Canadiana finally reached shore. Three more suspects were turned over by the ship's first mate and scores of victims were taken to hospital for treatment.

Scattered incidents continued to mar that summer, and there was a public outcry for action. New York Governor Averell Harriman voiced "grave concern" and Buffalo Mayor Stephen Pankow called civic meetings— and the passenger trade dropped like an anchor.

Just after Thanksgiving Day, with the Canadiana already laid up for the winter, the Crystal Beach Transit Co. announced that the Crystal Beach run would be discontinued. The stated reasons were competition from the automobile and the rising costs of steamboat operation. The Canadiana stayed at her dock through all of 1957.

In 1958, she was chartered to Seaway Excursion Lines to take passengers from Toledo, Ohio to Bob-Lo Island amusement park in the Detroit River. The Canadiana reached Toledo on May 25 and made her first run, to cheers, music and salutes, on May 30.

Just two months later, on July 30, the swing span of the Toledo Terminal Railroad Bridge closed in front of the excursion steamer and the Canadiana, whistles blowing and engines in reverse, hit the structure. Only three of the 885 passengers aboard suffered minor injuries, but the impact badly damaged the second and third decks from the bow to the superstructure salon bulkheads.

The summer cruises were cancelled, and in August, the federal courts seized the damaged vessel in a lawsuit filed to gain back wages for the 35-member crew. The Canadiana was appraised at $75,000 and sold at auction for $28,000 to a Seaway Excursion Lines director who formed a new company, Toledo Excursion Lines to run the ship.

Despite ice damage over the next winter, a remodelled Canadiana, with a sun deck at the bow where the damaged covered decks once were, was back on the Bob-Lo Island run. But in 1960 the vessel again was seized, this time in a bank foreclosure action against Toledo Excursion Lines.

The Lucas County Bank itself bought the boat at an auction that failed to attract bids anywhere near the appraised $80,000 value, and later in 1960 sold her to the newly-formed Pleasurama Excursion Line of Cleveland for service from Cleveland to the Cedar Point amusement park in Sandusky.

The Canadiana idled away 1961 and much of 1962 in Cleveland, as the plans fell through. On July 16, 1962 she once more reached Buffalo Harbor — at the end of a tow rope, heading for repairs at the Buffalo shipyards. But the shipyards closed, and the ship spent the rest of 1962, all of 1963, 1964, and 1965 and much of 1966 abandoned in a Rich marine dock while the artifacts were stripped and plans for shore-side restaurant or nightclub fell through.

In 1966 the boat was again sold, the Marina bills paid and the Pleasurama line dissolved. Her new owner, Sam Parella of Cleveland, had her towed to Fairport, Ohio, where she was sold twice before being towed to Cleveland — where the Canadiana was sold yet again, to Tropicana Products.

Tropicana, following a well-worn practice of trading in outmoded ships for better ships from the government's mothballed fleets, swapped the Canadiana for a chance to convert the former troop ship Gen. A.W. Greeley into an insulated orange juice tanker. The Canadiana wound up as a "shoe box vessel" owned by the U.S. Maritime Administration, barred by law from sailing and her tonnage traded in.

The vessel was sold for non-maritime use to a Cleveland restaurateur, Diamond Jim Vinci, for $36,000. But Diamond Jim, despite his years of work and thousands of dollars, failed to win city permits and his plans for a dockside nightclub fell through.

He leased the vessel in 1981 to two younger men, but they failed to pay the electric bills and power to the bilge pumps was cut off. When the Canadiana's growing list brought an open port hole down to the level of the Cuyahoga River, the aging steamer settled to the bottom at a spot known as Collision Bend.

The vessel stayed on the bottom for 15 months after the 1982 sinking. The Buffalo District of the Army Corps of Engineers awarded a $256,000 contract to Northrup Contracting of Brockport to raise the ship, and the Canadiana was refloated on May 13, 1983.

She was towed to Ashtabula, Ohio, where ownership was transferred to a newly-organized Buffalo group known as the "Friends of the Canadiana." Short on dollars but long on volunteer labor and nostalgia, the preservation group staged a series of fund-raising events and managed to make enough repairs to have the ship towed once more to Buffalo harbor.

The Canadiana reached Buffalo once more on September 17, 1984, to a salute from the fireboat, Edward M. Cotter. Crowds came to the Port of Buffalo to view the vessel and re-live memories, before the once-proud but badly deteriorated steamer was towed to the old Bell Slip for restoration work.

In December, 1985, a windstorm and a record eight-foot rise in water levels in eastern Lake Erie broke the Canadiana from her moorings and pushed her aground, but damage was limited to a broken rudder. More serious, by far, were the engineering estimates that put the cost of total restoration at more than $4.3 million—a sum the group is trying to raise one step at a time.

Through 1986, after a decision to try to restore the ship to sailing condition instead of undertaking a cosmetic, museum-type restoration, split the group's board of directors, dismantling of the vessel continued.

Photographs documented the work and the position of removed structural members, and paneling. The pilothouse and other key pieces were stored away for future use. Much of the rotted wood was scrapped, and the Canadiana was reduced to her hull, engine, main decking and the central structural stack.

In 1987, the Canadiana was moved once more. The stripped-down version of the former princess of the lakes was towed out of Buffalo Harbor and past Crystal Beach, to a new destination at a shipyard in Port Colborne, Ontario.

There she remained, as the 1980's drew to a close—her fate uncertain, but hope remaining that she might some day, once more be a part of the summers and magic on the Buffalo waterfront.

Coaster screams fill the air.
Courtesy of Buffalo State College, Courier Collection

"After the Memorial Day "Riots" of 1956…"

by Donald Golba

B ecause I was born in 1945, I had a few years to experience the wonders of the Canadiana. And experience them I did, because I don't recall sitting down for more than the first five minutes on those morning "outbound" trips. My mother had started her own tradition of taking me on the Crystal Beach Boat soon after school was let out for the summer. This was a once a year boat trip on a weekday while my father was at work. These trips were partly financed by my report card which could be taken to Loblaws to receive free ride-tickets, depending on how many A's and B's I had earned in my final report card for the year.

On that special morning we took the bus from Hertel Avenue to lower Main Street, an area considered by my parents as low-class, disreputable and not safe. Anyways, I was tense when we arrived at the wooden terminal building. As we purchased our tickets I wondered if we had missed the boat. But of course my mother was too smart to let that happen and we were usually early for everything. So we had time to board with other early arrivals and select the deck and side where we would sit. At eight years of age I had to sit until the boat cleared the breakwall and then I was allowed to explore the ship on my own. Watching the Buffalo skyline recede had lost my interest.

My mother cautioned me to take care and to report back to her and her girl friend. They had already shared with me their memories of the Starlight Ballroom and the music of the big bands that played there.

But I was interested in the boat itself and I loved the way she moved and rocked on the water. I was most interested in the moving parts of the engine that I saw through a screened area. I was awed to see the piston rods and crankshaft transmit their power to the propeller shaft. You could feel this power through your feet as the floor pulsated with the strokes of the engine. I held the railing and felt this rhythm with my whole body as the boat surged across the water. I welcomed the smells of the hot grease and oil for this was a wonderful steam engine and even a boy could see and understand how it worked. This was as close as it got to being in the belly of a great beast and its heartbeat thumped with massive power.

That power was transferred through the shaft to the propeller. Here in the stern, I watched the froth-filled wake of this powerful creation and felt the rhythm of its heartbeat. But there were more decks to explore before I reported back to mom. Then together we watched the outline come into

**Buffalo police are prepared for any further trouble aboard the Canadiana
- May 30, 1956.**
Courtesy of Buffalo State College, Courier Collection

view of the Comet roller coaster and the Canadian shore. Thanks mom for sharing this with me.

On the return trip to Buffalo we were tranquilized by the gentle roll of the boat. People pointed and shouted at the Buffalo skyline and landmarks. And I was anxious to tell my friends about this great adventure.

My last Canadiana ride was in 1955 after I finished the fourth grade. That winter my sister was born and I was no longer an only child. After the Memorial Day "Riot" in 1956, families stopped taking the boat and soon it was gone. Since then, I have traveled on many other boats but I miss most of all that engine room and wake of the Crystal Beach Boat.

My family and I continued to make many trips to Crystal Beach each year via the more mundane auto-route over the Peace Bridge in the family car. On almost every Saturday evening during the summer we introduced my sister to Kiddie Land. These trips always paused at The Fort Erie Race Track where my father made small wagers. Losing meant hot dogs and Loganberry at the walk-up hot dog stands on the street just outside the Crystal Beach Park. Winning meant repeat rides on The Giant Coaster with mom plus dinner at the Pines Restaurant.

Class Field Trip of 1959

By Donald Golba

'GEEZUS, WATCH OUT FOR THE NUNS!"

"Hey, look at this, our bus driver's plastered!" yelled one of the guys in the back of our bus. "Yeah, he's all over the road, I just seen us go over the yellow lines." We sprang to the windows to confirm this as our eighth grade class left Crystal Beach on our return trip home to Buffalo. After a couple minutes of weaving, the bus slowed down and got steadier as Sister Mary bent his ear. She was our teacher- nun and chaperone. And she either scared the crap out of him or put the fear of God into him. Just as she was able to do to her Catholic school students. But hey it worked and the forty angelic boys and girls would return safely to their families who expected them home for supper.

Those were the days well before M.A.D.D. (Mothers Against Drunk Drivers) What else could occupy the middle-aged driver for 6 hot sunny hours while he waited to return us to Buffalo? I think the shady coolness of the hotel tap-room was too much for him to pass up. No doubt this was against company policy but us guys thought it was way- cool at the time and a great story to tell on the street corner.

In the back of the bus, we still had the problem of hiding illicit fireworks on our persons so as not to arouse the notice of the United States Immigration and Customs inspectors. Davie had just been clued-in. For the first time, he realized he needed to conceal half a shopping bag of contraband-fireworks, a major investment of several dollars.

We decided he should sit in the far back corner. What he couldn't hide in his clothes he should stash on the floor behind his feet. The biggest guy would sit in front of him and cover him as much as possible. Luckily the inspector followed last year's procedure. He walked down the aisle and looked you in the eye.

Each kid blurted out only one word of two syllables: "Buf-flow." This was in answer to the question, "Where were you born?" Our answers confirmed citizenship in our glorious democracy, the land of the free and the home of the brave, from which eighth grade boys could travel to a foreign land, smoke cigars like real men and smuggle explosives back to our homeland.

Yep, earlier that day after lunch, the four of us shared two cigars in the park picnic-grove as planned for a week. "GEEZUS, WATCH OUT FOR THE NUNS!" Davie said as he lit up the first one. I think he was the one who had snitched them from his father. We passed the two cigars in our little circle.

"Wow, these sure taste great," we said to each other. But our faces showed otherwise. Actually about this time I would have preferred an ice cream cone and I believe the others would have too. But I had my honor to uphold and saying that I would have preferred ice cream would have gotten me mocked-out. We finally ditched our stinky cigars. And after some quiet-time, our heads cleared and our digestive tracts returned to normal. Now we could go back and hit the Midway with our remaining tickets.

To a pre-teen boy, the second coolest ride at Crystal Beach after the Comet was the "Dodge-'Em-Bumper Cars." Smiling spectators lined the outer railings and the line-up of riders confirmed the popularity of this ride. Younger children that couldn't meet the height requirement were still fascinated with the bump and crash action. But many of the rides outside of Kiddie Land had signs next to the ticket-taker with a prominent horizontal line painted on it. Above or below the line were the words, "You must be this tall to ride." As you handed him your ticket, the attendant gave you a glance. Most kids knew their heights and saved themselves the embarrassment of rejection. Once in a while a kid would be stopped and he would stand on his tip-toes as the attendant glanced down and barked, "Nope, you're too young!" A kid with head- hung low was turned away in defeat.

The object of this ride was to bump the other drivers as hard as you could. The bumper-car had a sturdy metal-screened border topped by an armpit high railing. It ran on a slippery metal floor while overhead was a metal ceiling that carried the electricity that powered the bumper cars below.

I had a couple years experience on this ride sharpening my skills. My preferred target was a woman driver that couldn't handle her car. If she was pretty and shrieked loudly she would attract me along with a pack of other guys. We showed no mercy.

At 12 years of age, I also hunted the more skilled drivers, especially the older guys trying to look cool among their friends. You earned his respect if you blind-sided or tee-boned him hard on a turn. But this meant that he had your number and would be out for revenge. With a big smile on my face I sped away and tried to stay ahead of him. As I ran into the next pile up I knew what was coming. Yep, he got me back with a vicious thump and it was all part of the fun. Grudges were left in your car as you climbed out of it and happily slid your way to the exit.

The cool teenage boy's uniform was a bright white tee- shirt, long hair slicked back with Brylcream or Wild Root Cream Oil. Careful grooming created an Elvis-look that was complimented by pointed black shoes or motorcycle boots. Blue Levi denims polished the image. Many guys also carried a pack of cigs rolled up in a tee-shirt sleeve. Later in the evening there were guys who wore gang-colors on their jacket or vest. That was my signal to stay clear of them. I was lucky when my mother let me wear blue jeans that my father called overalls and some people called dungarees.

Ride tickets bought at the tiny ticket booths inside the park cost six cents each. If you went with a school or your neighborhood business association then the tickets cost four cents each. The savvy shopper also could purchase tickets for four cents at local store promotions in Buffalo. For the most part I heard people order tickets in batches of two or three dollars. Anyone with fifty or sixty tickets could go on a lot of rides.

The tamer rides like the Caterpillar, the Merry-Go-Round and the Ferris wheel were two tickets a ride. There were a number of three ticket rides. Four tickets, 24 cents if you paid full price, got you on the more exciting rides like the Giant Coaster, the Wild Mouse, and the Dodge-Em-bumper cars. The ultimate thrill ride of the North-East and in a class by itself, the Comet cost five tickets in the fifties and may have gone to six tickets later on. Such was its fearsome reputation among us that few seventh and eighth graders rode it then, even though many could meet the height requirement. I would save it for another time and ride it after a year in high school.

There was never an admission charge at the gates until years later. And you were free to exit the park to the summer resort town of Crystal Beach. There were a couple of candy or variety stores that sold newspapers, candy, cigarettes, and fireworks. We were amazed to see that the candy bars and cigarettes were all different brands from ours in Buffalo. We admired the packs of "Players" cigarettes in their royal green packages with a colorful picture of a British sailor in the middle. We never tested Canadian law by trying to buy cigarettes but they did sell us fireworks because what we did with them was our own business, even though they must have known we were Americans.

Notice that two or three bucks got you a lot in 1959. Even in the sixties you could nearly fill up your car with two or three dollars worth of regular gas. I was stung by inflation when candy bars at our local corner store went from a nickel to a dime in one year, a 100% increase! In the park, some people spent a lot of money at the game booths to win a cheap prize. But those cheap, big prizes sure looked impressive as some lucky winners carried them around the park. That helped drum up business.

The food stands inside the park only accepted tickets as their currency. This meant that people leaving the park with leftover tickets could load up on sugar waffles and Hall's famous suckers to take home. Each huge sucker cost only one ticket and could easily last the entire ride to the Peace Bridge.

Crystal Beach was the only place that I ever saw Loganberry sold. A

TILT-A-WHIRL.
Rick Herbert Collection

sweet purple drink sold at the hot dog stands. Charcoal broiled hot dogs cost a quarter and ice cream cones cost a dime. An icy cold bottle of Coca-Cola also cost a dime. I am holding one of these classic curved bottles as I write this piece. I had to confirm that they held only 6 ounces and not 8 ounces. Imagine that, we were satisfied with a drink of only 6 ounces.

Much like Crystal Beach itself, things were smaller then but better. If you ever experienced the park in the past, go back to the site and see for yourself how few acres contained so much magic. The big hill of sand that the small train ride disappeared around is still there as well as the huge pier built for all the excursion boats that brought so many patrons over the years. The white sandy beach is still being used by day bathers.

My class was the first of the "Baby Boom" generation and many of us would enter the military during the Vietnam War. We had been tested by our peers on the streets of Buffalo. And Crystal Beach was our summer playground.

Look Out World! "The Sixties" was our oyster and the times they were a-changin.

"The smell of that hot and gooey candy being fed into the sucker machine was heavenly."

Jim Murphy, Richmond Virginia

My family had a summer cottage one half block from the park. At night as a boy I fell asleep to the screams of the happy Giant coaster riders and to the mournful, lonely call of the Point Abino foghorn.

As a kid, 9 to12 years old and living so close to the park, we knew which days of the week they would make the Carmel Corn, the Taffy Kisses, and most of all the Halls Suckers! The smell of that candy, hot and gooey, being fed into the sucker-making machine was heavenly.

The candy sucker machine was a three-person operation. The hot mass was blended in a dough-mixer machine and then extruded by hand by the candy maker who would feed the snake like goodness into this rickety old, clanking machine. A stick was placed on a conveyor belt and the sucker was stamped onto the stick. The next guy in line was a kid, 15 to16 years old, whose job it was to stand close to where the suckers came out of the stamper. If one came out without a stick or deformed, he'd grab the candy and place it back into the hot candy mass to be re-cast. In addition, this guy had a large screwdriver which he would use to whack the string of suckers, every 8 or 9 as they passed, so they could be placed on a tray to cool. At the end of the long conveyor belt, maybe 20 feet away, was the last person in the operation. At the end, the candy had already begun to cool and harden. Then the suckers were placed on cookie trays to finish cooling before final separation and sale.

Not all that much of a story, except that if you stood around and watched the operation, it was best to stand near the guy with the screwdriver. If he got backed up and he could not get the deformed candy back into the hot goo, he had to dispose of that morsel, hot, gooey and indescribably delicious! He'd give it to the closest kid who just stood and watched. Wonderful! Slurp, yum, yum. But it was important to know about the sucker-making schedule.

Remember, I was a summer resident. My family lived about one half block from the park entrance. Every year, the day after school was dismissed, we'd move to the beach and stay until the day after Labor Day.

Many of the Buffalo companies would have their company picnics at Crystal Beach. When we were 9-10 years old it was common for the local kids, American and Canadian, to show up at the stadium for company games. Most of us had a genuine affection for the pie-eating contest. We were all winners! Many firms would have races, balloon toss and greased pig chases for the kids. My cousin Dan was always very fast, and would always win or place in the 100 yard dash (no meters in those days you know).

The Master of Ceremonies would get Dan up on the podium to present him the prize and would say, " Well Dan, where's your family?" And Dan would point into the stands and sometimes even wave to a non- existent parent for a ring of authenticity. "And where does your dad work son?" And Dan would say "maintenance." Everyone had a maintenance department. In truth, of course, Dan's father was a plumber who worked construction and never went to any company picnic.

At the age of about 12-14 we'd spend a good part of each day at Tommy Dillon's pony track. At that time it was located at the base of the stadium next to the parking lot and just outside the park proper. We'd scoop manure and walk around the track holding the really young kids from falling from the old and very gentle ponies, many of which were never burdened with a saddle. There must've been six or eight of us hangers-on every day, doing drudge work and working for free, but early in the morning, after the ponies had been fed, we saddled the frisky ponies and we would be allowed an hour or so to ride the spirited ponies on the beach or through the fields. That hour or so far made up for any free labor and smelly clothing. What kid wouldn't want a pony to ride?

Crystal Beach was a perfect location for professional wrestlers to settle in for the summer. It was a short ride to Buffalo, Niagara Falls, Toronto or Hamilton for the matches each week. I was enormously pleased to live next door to a rental cottage that hosted wrestlers each year.

My favorite was Tex MacKenzie who at the time was world tag team champion with Whipper Billy Watson of Toronto. Tex was great to me as a kid. We'd go together to Windmill Quarry off the Dominion Highway so I could swim and he'd work out with the weights that he'd keep in his car trunk. On the way home we'd stop at the Crystal Beach Dairy and he'd buy us the highest ice cream cones you could imagine. Each day he'd challenge the waitress to try to pile "one more scoop" on top of what seemed to be a mountain of ice cream.

Tex and Billy lost the championship that summer to the Togo Brothers, who also lived in Crystal Beach. The Togo's were also nice to us kids and gave many of us the very first flip-flops we'd ever seen. They were not available in stores at that time so if you had them, you were definitely cool!

But I was torn between the Togo's and Tex. I mean the Togo's were O.K. but Tex was my friend. Tex shared ice cream and he'd been out sailing with my Dad and me. We kept a 21' Lightning sailboat that my Dad had built, on the property of my Dad's boss at Point Abino. Where was my loyalty?

I became even more confused one day shortly after Tex and Billy had lost that coveted belt. I rode my bike past the Togo's home. There they were, the evil and enemy Togo's. They were drinking a beer in the driveway with my friend Tex! The entire world failed to make sense to this ten year old!

In addition to Tex and the Togo's we were befriended by other wrestlers such as The Mighty Urses, Roberto Pico, The Brunetti Brothers and Sky High Lee.

When not at the pony track or later at a real job, our free time was spent at the beach. As a youngster, when the Canadiana made her regular departure back to Buffalo at two, four and six, we'd swim out next to the dock and dive for pennies, nickels and dimes. Quarters were rare in those days and as exciting to catch as a doubloon. After the crowd left we'd dig in the soft sand for coins nobody had caught. We'd usually "earn" enough for French fries, a pack of cigarettes (a big mistake as I later learned) and a few games on our favorite pinball machine at the arcade. We'd stay in the water until we turned blue but also turned a tidy profit. What more could you ask for?

While at the beach, as a fifteen-eighteen year old, it was status to lay your blanket next to the lifeguard stand. The closer you actually got to that stand, of course, the higher the status. The guards were always nice to us and yet very conscientious about their jobs. My recollection was that Crystal Beach had an outstanding safety record at the beach.

A few perks accrued to those of us who were befriended by the lifeguards. If the beach was not busy or if it was time to replace the guard "on the block" we'd get to row the lifesaving boat out, just for fun or to transfer guards. The "block" of course was the concrete diving platform situated about even with the boarding area of the Crystal Beach Boat.

A few days a year it would be cloudy and cold and there would be very few swimmers. On those days a bunch of us, with most of the lifeguards, would play touch football on the beach -- all day long! This was again a joint adventure with both Canadians and Americans involved. I remember two lifeguards, Billy and Jimmy who played college ball at Ohio State. They were huge. I remember much younger Canadian kids like Terry and Pete who at fourteen competed pretty evenly with the eighteen year old guys, despite the age difference.

The best perk, however, was the day after Labor Day. The park was now closed until next year. The lifeguards would collect hot dogs, burgers, sodas, chips, and ice cream from the now closed concession stands and host a party on the beach for all of us whose blankets were closest to the guard stand. The guards didn't get paid for that day; they just did it for us. That might have been the best day each summer.

At the end of summer, few but residents will remember the annual parade and burial. Crystal Beach was a great spot for cottages rented to high school fraternities and sororities. Each Labor Day, from the mid 1950's, it was a tradition for the fraternities and sororities to hold a parade beginning in Queens Circle, past Hot Dog Alley and down Erie Road to Ridge Road, later Ridgeway Road, then down to "stink beach." That's the beach on the opposite side of the Comet, not in the park. At that point they would bury in the sand a makeshift coffin -- that was the ceremony to bury summer. The summer romances, the fun, the memories would lay buried in the sands of Crystal Beach where I suspect they remain today.

As a summer kid, there was one place to go at night. Only one place, every night, every single night! We had our own corner. The Swing Inn on Erie Road near Bay Beach was the place. On one side an arcade, the other a hot dog stand, and in the center, behind walls but open to the sky above, was a pink concrete dance floor. We would see some of the very best jitterbugging that would rival the regulars on American Bandstand. Again, this was a collection of Americans and Canadians, but almost completely those of us who lived at the Beach.

I could be there, even as my little sister and her friends were nearby (ugh) and suffer no embarrassment! We would all collect and enjoy dancing to Rock n Roll and savor the warm summer nights. Then if you were lucky enough to get a "yes" for a "clutch and grabber" (slow dance) with a really cute chick, well life couldn't get any better. Some popular songs and/or dances that I recall are "the Twist", "the Hand Jive", "Finger Poppin Time", "Quarter to Three" by Gary Bonds and anything by Elvis or Bobby Darrin. Of course you better not show up before 9:30 p.m. -- not too cool. The place closed at 11:30 p.m., the same as the park. We were free to roam the village even after midnight (no curfews). It was hard to get in trouble then and completely safe to be out and about.

Around that time we had friends who worked at the Crystal Beach Bathhouse. We'd go there for a moonlight swim, after the boat left and the park had closed. This was as much fun as anything else we'd do. Our friends would open up the bathhouse and we'd use the rental swim suits -- girls to the Ladies side, boys to the Men's side. I recall no hanky panky -- a disappointment to some of us.

I guess if I thought about it some more I'd have other memories. Others will recall the rides, the Comet in particular, perhaps a long lost love, the carefree and uncomplicated lives we used to live. For me Crystal Beach is more than a place or a distant memory. It is a wonderful part of my life that lives within me every day.

Auto Scooter Bumper Cars.
Rick Herbert Collection

Laughing Sal.
Cathy Herbert Collection

Helene and daughter Cathy
taken in a photo booth in Crystal Beach Park.

La P'tite (Little) Helene
"She made the caramel corn, cotton candy and candy apples."

Andre Germain

Mom barely spoke a word of English. We'd moved to Welland from Rouyn, Quebec in May 1951 and in 1959 our father abandoned us. That's why she had to get a job to support us. I was 16, my sister Louise was 15, my brother Michel was 8 and my baby sister Cathy was 2 years old.

Mom worked at Crystal Beach Park for 29 years in the stand between the Magic Carpet and the Laff In The Dark. She was there from 1960 until 1989 when the park closed down. She made all the caramel corn for the various stands in the park, as well as the "cotton candy" and candy apples. She sold candy kisses as well. She worked eleven and a half hour shifts from 12 noon until closing which was usually 11:30 p.m., seven days a week. Everybody knew her as "la p'tite Helene" ("Little Helen"). She was an "institution there, in the employ of George Hall and later, his son Ed and she was paid a whopping 26 cents an hour.

Often she worked right through her lunch break and her coffee breaks when the park was really busy with many company picnics. The park was one of a kind in the whole of northeastern North America and many companies such as Westinghouse, Atlas Steels, Electromet, Stokes Rubber, etc., had their company picnics there. She never charged the Halls for that extra time that she worked.

The Halls hired two men to prepare the caramel corn. Unfortunately, those two guys were slackers and often shirked their duties and headed for one of the local bars. When the park got busy and the caramel corn started running short, Ma would take over the chore, pouring the ingredients into that big vat, cooking and stirring the works with a big, heavy wooden paddle.

Man's work. And Ma was only 4'8" and weighed about 95 lbs. soaking wet! And she was already in her late 40's, closing on 50. After covering for these men on many occasions, the Halls finally found out what was going on. They fired the two men and "generously" offered Ma 10 cents more an hour to take care of the caramel corn as well.

My mother lived in Welland and never learned to drive a car. She managed to get rides to work at the park anyway she could. Often that meant hitchhiking with her youngest daughter, Cathy, who at the time was pre-school age. Ma managed to land jobs at the park for a lot of people over the years. She was smart enough to make sure that these people had cars so that she would be assured a ride to work. In spite of all the hardships, Ma never missed a day of work at the park in all the years that she worked there.

Helene also worked as a chambermaid at the Rose Villa every morning until eleven and then went straight from there to Crystal Beach to put in a 12-hour day. Then in late summer, she'd get a job at a canning factory in St. Davids, working the midnight shift, leaving from Crystal Beach to go directly to the canning factory and then start all over again at the Rose Villa the next morning. This woman kept up this routine every summer, 7 days a week for years! She worked untold hours with no sleep except the dozing she'd do for a few minutes while in transit between jobs.

She got me a job there on that "Looper" in 1961. My sisters and then my nieces all worked there too. My sister Cathy (the one my mother had in tow hitchhiking) worked there in her teens in Ma's stand and met her husband-to-be, Bob Roberts, there at the park. A Crystal Beach resident, Bob also worked at the park for a few years.

Often kids would not have enough tickets to buy cotton candy or other treats, but Helene gave it to them anyway and made up the price difference out of her own pocket. Plus, when the park started to charge admission, Helene would talk to the gate people and get them to allow friends and family into the park, free of charge. She bent the ear of ride operators to allow free rides for poor kids who could not afford the rides. Poor kids also received complimentary candy kisses, caramel corn and cotton candy from Helene.

Near Helene's stand was this grotesque plastic mock-up of a huge fat lady called Laughing Sal. This abomination had a continuous laugh-track that roared a raucous "Ha Ha Ha Ha Ha Ha Ha!" Sal was a constant source of irritation to me for the whole summer that I worked at the Looper. I wanted to rip down that gross, cackling witch and kill her voice forever. To this day, I can't understand how Helene managed to work near that cacophonous hyena all those years and still retain her sanity.

The park had its seedy side with the carny attractions and the con games that offered prizes such as giant Teddy Bears, just waiting to take a shills hard-earned money. These carny types would do anything for a buck and in the summer of 1962, I tried to have as little to do with them as possible. Helene, on the other hand, in her charming non-judgmental naiveté, never saw that seediness and treated them the same as anybody else. Some of them would hit her up for money for a meal and she never refused if she had any money available. Consequently, even those con artists grew to respect la p'tite Helene. So, even though a few may have taken advantage of her generosity, most of them made sure to repay her kindness.

When the park closed in 1989 and all its contents were auctioned off, Helene broke down in tears. To her it was the end of her summer vacations, her chance to go to a place where she could see all her old friends and meet new people on a daily basis. Working at Crystal Beach Amusement Park was the one job that she loved. In the years following its closure, anytime she saw anything to remind her of the park, her eyes grew misty. When PBS aired that program about the park, "Things That Aren't There Any More," she had a hard time watching it. A very happy part of her life had come to an end.

Helene died in June 2004 at 89 years of age. Her family held a celebration of her life a couple of weeks later, at her apartment on Riverside Drive in Welland where she had lived since 1960. Hundreds of people showed up at that tiny apartment and we were flooded with happy memories of "la p'tite Helene," the lady who got many of these people their first jobs.

On the Scrambler. Estimate of 9,000 people at Crystal Beach for Kenmore Merchants Day and Genessee-Pine Hill Business Mens' Association Annual Picnic, June 27, 1963.

Courtesy of Buffalo State College, Courier Collection

Charles F. Dowd, Inc
240 Huron Street
Toledo 4, Ohio

For: Lucas County Bank
515 Madison Avenue
Toledo 4, Ohio

FOR IMMEDIATE RELEASE
S.S. Canadiana
Toledo – June 3, 1960

Time, the tide and mortgage payments will run out next Monday (June 13) for the S.S. Canadiana, the last of the excursion boats of its kind on the Great Lakes offering moonlight and daytime cruises during the summer for excursionists.

She goes under the auctioneer's hammer of the United States Marshal at 10 a.m. to satisfy an unpaid mortgage of $30,000 held by Lucas County Bank here.

The vessel was ordered seized by U.S. District Judge Frank L. Kloeb on April 20 following foreclosure action started by the bank.

She has since been appraised at $52,000 for salvage purposes and at $80,000 as a going concern.

"It is the intention of the bank to bid the vessel in the hopes she may be preserved for the excursion trade," J.M. LaPorte, executive vice president for the Lucas County Bank, said.

The vessel, which came to Toledo from Buffalo, N.Y., in 1958, was completely remodelled last year. The third deck forward was removed and the second deck forward converted to a sun deck. The vessel, which is a 3-decker, is certified to carry 2,500 passengers and a crew of 34.

There are cocktail lounges on the first deck and on the third and a dance floor on the second deck.

The vessel was built in Buffalo in 1910 and until 1958 was the property of The Crystal Transport Co., offering excursions between that city and Crystal Beach on the Canadian side.

She was purchased in 1958 by a group of Detroit residents operating as Seaway Excursion Lines.

In 1959, she was bought by a group composed chiefly of Toledoans known as Toledo Excursion Lines.

Under both ownerships, the ship made daily trips to Bob-Lo Island, located at the mouth of the Detroit River. There were also nightly trips into Lake Erie.

Her registered length is 209.7 feet; breath, 45 feet with a depth of 15.8 feet. Registered tonnage is 974 tons gross and 427 net.

Philip Thorpe was captain of the vessel in 1958 and Joseph Wiepert her master last year.

98

The Canadiana's pilothouse with the ship's wheel was the brain center for operating the Crystal Beach Boat. Wind, waves and shallow water complicated the task of arrivals and departures. Thousands of passengers anxiously watched the boat's progress while it was hampered by limited space to maneuver.

Courtesy of Buffalo State College, Courier Collection

"My husband made-out with girls on the midnight ride..."
"I was seven months pregnant on the Comet coaster."

Carol Hess

Crystal Beach goes way back in my family. Not only did my grandparents have a house at Erie Beach (Jens and Francis Christensen) but also our family camped at Sherkston Quarry. What more could a girl ask for? Our summer days were spent at Erie Beach in Fort Erie or Sherkston. At least twice a week our evenings were spent at Crystal. There I dated Canadian and American guys. But I have a special place in my heart for the Canadian guys.

Regarding Crystal, my dad helped build the Cyclone roller coaster. It was really dangerous if you didn't weigh enough and didn't hold on tight. You could be lifted right out of your seat!

I remember going on the new Comet coaster when I was seven months pregnant. It was the day Robert Kennedy was shot. We didn't know it happened until we returned home that evening. The operator didn't see that I was pregnant until my 4th or 5th ride. He nearly had a heart attack when he saw me and he wouldn't let me back on! What a bummer!

My future father-in-law worked part-time in the engine room of the Crystal Beach Boat when he wasn't working at Republic Steel. My future sister-in-law worked in the Crystal Beach office in Buffalo as a secretary and in payroll. And my future husband worked in the concession stands on the boat and as a crewmember when needed.

When the Hess family members worked for Crystal Beach in the late 1940's and 50's and until the riots, the Hall family owned and operated the Park. The Hess family knew the Halls fairly well as they had worked for them over the years. One of my sister-in laws was very close to the family.

My husband who is now 65 had the perfect job as a teenager working as a crewmember and working in the concession stands on the boat. He was able to make-out with the girls on the midnight/last ride to Buffalo. He would take the girls to the upper deck where it was off limits to the passengers. He said it was better than the Tunnel of Love. If you are approximately his age, I'm sure that you can appreciate being able to do that in the 1950's. I'm almost 6 years younger than my husband and was too young to date him when he was 17 and 18. That's why I never made it to the top deck.

Our families knew each other since we lived in the same neighborhood called the Fruit Belt. He went to Seneca with my oldest brother and I went to P.S. 37 with my sister. I had a crush on my future husband when I was 12. But

100

he was not interested in me other than to say "Hi" to me when I met my brother and him after school at the bus stop. My family then moved to North Buffalo/Central Park Plaza area. And we didn't meet again until he walked into the Mansion House when I was 20 years old. Then he was interested.

My husband has tons of stories, not only about the girls he met, but experiences of working on the Crystal Beach Boat. The Captain had a chef who supposedly was a chef for the Czar of Russia. The Captain liked to eat and the crew was fed whatever the Captain had, so the crew ate well. But sometimes entrees were too exotic for a teenager from Buffalo's Fruit Belt! My husband said he didn't try some of the food because it was so unfamiliar, mostly seafood. He now regrets this except for the squid and octopus!

He said a feast was prepared for the crew 3 times a day. Breakfast offered anything you wanted, ham, bacon, sausage. Eggs were done to your taste with muffins, rolls, and toasts. Lunches were the main meal of the day with soups and entrees of all sorts with every kind of vegetable and side dish and always ended with all types of desserts, from plain to fancy. Dinners were always hot but there were also cold sandwiches of various types with fruit, condiments and desserts again.

And, if by chance you were hungry during/after the evening runs, there was more food. He said he didn't understand how the company could afford to feed the Captain and crew in such a grand way. And then count the rolls at the concession stands to keep track of how many hotdogs were sold. If he didn't eat what the chef prepared, he would eat the Sahlen's wieners without rolls. Otherwise, a wiener with a roll would have cost him money.

My husband worked the day the riots occurred on board, but he refused to work the later runs that day. He said the previous runs of the day were bad enough with smaller fights, knives and taunting. He felt things were not going to get any better as the day went on and he was allowed to take the rest of the day off. The boat was a little short-handed. As my husband remembers it, only passengers staying in Canada were allowed aboard in Buffalo for the last return trip. The boat owners had decided that the last round trip had to be completed to pick up customers that otherwise would be stranded at Crystal Beach...the rest is history! The decision to curtail passengers to those only staying in Canada on the trip over was viewed as racist.

For years, the Crystal Beach Boat Company had a contract to deliver and pick-up mail daily between Buffalo and Crystal Beach during the season, even if bad weather did not allow passengers. My husband said that the boat made at least one daily trip to do so. He would work these runs, as they usually were not too bad. That is until he went through a storm that he swears would sink or capsize the boat. He said that there were waves so high that they went over the top of the top deck. There was no kidding between crewmembers on board that day. They all thought they were going to die. After they made it ashore, the words of the song, "The Edmund Fitzgerald" rang true in their ears and haunted them during future trips. Even now during storms, he still hums that tune. I miss Crystal. It was a special place.

As for Sherkston, there was an old shipwreck off the Sherkston shore. We always wanted to swim out to it but were afraid of getting caught in the undertow…there was a wicked one that had drowned a friend who used to hang out at Pleasant Beach. We did canoe out to the wreck once but never went aboard.

We liked to sit on the rocks along side the eternal gas leak that was aflame between Empire and Elco Beach. I wonder how many people knew about the natural gas leak and whether it still is there? We would sit on the rocks and tell stories about how the shipwreck occurred. Sort of like telling ghost stories around a campfire.

My family knew Mr. Holman, the man who owned Sherkston Quarry and beaches. It cost .25 cents a night to camp there in the sand dunes near where the "new" concrete showers/restrooms were built. These replaced the old wood change room between the entrance and the Snack Shack. The original change room was a one room wooden shack on short stilts that the crew repositioned every spring.

When Mr. Holman built the "new" restrooms and then made the parking lot bigger, we moved our camping site over to the cemetery. Many people didn't know the cemetery was there. A fence in the middle of what is called Fiddler's Green now encloses it.

In the 50's and 60's we were camping there in tents with some of the Schneider family. They were the original first campers at Sherkston. There were no fences and we used to threaten the little kids camping with us that if they didn't behave, we would put them in the cemetery at night and leave them. There were still many tombstones dating back to a diphtheria epidemic at the turn of the century. They had homes on the other side of the quarry. Some of their foundations were still there in the 50's and early 60's. And, yes there is a train of sorts at the bottom of the quarry. It brought the stone out of the quarry. It was left there when the quarry stopped operating.

I remember Lee the lifeguard who was a gym teacher at Riverside High School. He would scuba dive down to the train and the old shack at the bottom of the quarry.

During the 1970's, when Sherkston and Wildewood were wild with drugs, people would take the tombstones to use with their tent stakes or to level their campers. It was a shame, since most of the tombstones disappeared along with the lilac and evergreen trees planted around the graves.

We didn't camp too much at Sherkston during the 70's until our sons were old enough to swim there and to be cautious around water. Then we camped alongside the frog pond at the end of Fiddler's Green. We would sit outside near the corner and watch the police bust the kids with drugs. It was quite a lesson for my pre-teen and teenage sons. They never tried drugs as far as we know.

It was exciting to sit on the rocks on the beach and watch a storm come in. The dark clouds rolled in across the bright, blue sky. The lake came alive with gentle breaths that swelled into a roar. Then huge waves crashed at the rocks below our feet. We'd scream. It was so exhilarating -- this majesty of nature!

"... when the Canadiana would rock from one side to another."

George Hutchings

I'm over 70 years old now, but when I was a young man I used to drive into Buffalo and park my old car and get a round trip ticket on the Canadiana to Crystal Beach. I loved to go on rough and windy days when the boat would rock from one side to another. I saw the slot machines in action on the boat, but I was too young to gamble.

"... the virgin and the dynamo."

Michael Joyce, Meditations

Below deck there was a snack bar which, for economic reasons, we were never allowed to patronize. The main attraction there was a view of the engine room and the huge brass piston turning on a thick black arm. It was the Crystal Beach Boat that came to mind when I first read Henry Adam's account of the virgin and the dynamo. We would watch the huge arm and the piston for moments on end, but then rush up the iron staircase to the deck when the park came into focus in the glare of sunshine above the horizon.

Leo, The Paper Eater.
Cathy Herbert Collection

"I'm Leo the Lion - The Paper Eater... Please Feed Me."

Drew Bell

In the summer of 1966 I was 13 years old and I worked in the Canteen at Crystal Beach as a Bus Boy. I brought burgers, salads, and coffee to the pavilions where the big American plants were having Family Day. We wore blue uniforms with little pillbox hats. We were paid a dollar an hour but one dollar was deducted from each paycheck in order to cover the cost of the food that we ate. We were allowed to eat as much food as we wanted and I could easily eat 8 burgers per day.

One of my memories of the Canteen was working near a trash kiosk that had a lion's head with a vacuum mouth. That Lion bellowed a message ad nauseum to people who put paper into its mouth, "I'm Leo The Lion... The Paper Eater...Please Feed Me" I heard this message so often that I prayed that someone would kidnap Leo and ship him back to the jungle. But he did serve his purpose. Kids would come from a great distance with a variety of garbage and let Leo inhale the stuff.

104

Occasionally I was sent to Kiddie Land to help as a ticket taker and to make sure that the kids were secured in their seats.

In the summer of 1967 I saw real hippies for the first time, guys with shoulder length hair and girls with hairy legs and long dresses. Their clothes would have been fashionable when Crystal Beach first opened at the turn of the century. And their aroma was as old as Crystal Beach and was definitely not that of waffles or Old Spice.

As a teenager in the late 1960's we could easily hitchhike to Crystal on the weekend. With free admission to the Park we could still enjoy rides with just a few dollars to spare. The Comet and Wild Mouse came first but we soon changed our pattern. First we would ride on the Skyride that went out over the lake. While high in the air we would smoke a jay and be really high when we touched the ground. That's when we went directly to the Comet coaster next door and got totally blown away.

We would walk through the Park and stop to talk to a friend who ran the Roll-O-Plane. We would have a free ride for an extended period of time. This was fun until you rolled in the air for 15 minutes and then screamed at him to stop.

Before the Derby Street riot, I remember the rows of motorcycles parked under the Giant coaster. The bikers were all milling around freaking out the oldsters and impressing the shit out of wannabe hoodlums like myself. These Black Diamond Riders and The Para Dice Riders were there together. I never saw them on any of the rides. They just walked around and menaced people. Without helmets they also rode their choppers up and down Derby Road past the Loganberry Bar.

In the early 1980's the Park was struggling to survive. As a Friday night promotion they had CAR LOAD NIGHT. All the people that you could stuff into a car got into the Park for a total of $19.95. At the time I drove a '69 Mercury Marquis that I would pack with daughters, nephews, nieces and neighborhood kids. Then we had a grand evening on all the rides for a measly 20 bucks.

The paint was faded and chipped, the trees overgrown and the workers seemed like second-class carny rejects. But Crystal Beach Park was a big part of my personal history and will remain a fond memory to me. How marvelous it must have been in its heyday.

Push the pedal to the metal to loop the Looper during Hertel-North Park and East Aurora Community Day, June 26, 1963.
Courtesy of Buffalo State College, Courier Collection

"— my seven year old daughter was thrown from the ride from a height of forty feet!"

Janet Truckenbrodt

My memories of Crystal Beach Amusement Park can best be described as bittersweet. That which gives the most joy may also give the most sorrow. This was the case of my family's relationship with the Park. Our story spans most of the 20th century.

I was born in 1926 in Crystal Beach just after the completion of the famous Crystal Ballroom and the infamous Cyclone roller coaster. My American mother Helen and Canadian father Charles had a home within walking distance of the Park. Here they raised sister Ruth, brother Fred and me.

Growing up in Crystal Beach during the first half of the century could be compared to a vacation in Disney World for three months of the year. Excitement filled the air. From 11 a.m. until midnight, the clang of the rides, the screams of the riders and the shriek from the whistle of the S.S. Canadiana echoed throughout the village.

For the handful of permanent residents of the Village of Crystal Beach, the Amusement Park was a great source of summer employment. For our family, the Park was our only means of support. My father trained under his father and grandfather and was in charge of all the painting and decorating for the entire park. His office was in the basement of the ballroom and served as his laboratory for creating the multitude of colors that adorned every structure in the midway. Pre-mixed paints were not available at that time. The cars for the rides were painted during the fall and winter in the ballroom. All 20,000 square feet of that beautiful dance floor had to be covered with canvas tarps before the painting began.

My family's link to the Park was unique because all five of us worked there in one capacity or another. My brother Fred worked at the three main attractions in the Park, the sand beach, the Crystal Ballroom and the S.S. Canadiana. He started his day at 5.a.m. with a pick and rake cleaning the bathing beach. From there he moved to the dance hall to clean, wax and polish the exquisite floor. At 11.am and every two hours there after, he acted as a linesman for the mooring of the Canadiana. In the evenings, except on Sunday, he acted as an usher and ticket-taker in the dance hall. All this in one day!

In the 1930's, my sister Ruth sold Park tickets locked inside one of the distinctive booths. In the 1940's I got the higher status job of selling tickets inside the dance hall. Tickets were 10 cents each or 3 for 25 cents and were dispensed automatically by a push of a button— if you knew how to load the machine. While earning money I enjoyed the big band music of Bert Niosi, Harold Austin and Maynard Ferguson, the succession of local bands who played nightly.

After my father's death in 1952, my mother sold tickets for many years. She loved to talk about the variety of incidents she witnessed every day. She helped many families find lost children and became an information center for the Park as she sidestepped male admirers.

Those of us who lived in Crystal Beach during the first half of the 20th century were the privileged people. We experienced the golden years of the Park's history. Plus, American summer visitors and Canadian permanent residents became life long friends. Time cannot erase the sound of the big band music. Nothing can dull the thrill of the Cyclone, the Comet, the Caterpillar, the Tumblebug, the Ferris Wheel, the Wild Mouse or the surprises of the Fun House, the Laff in the Dark and the Magic Carpet. We will never forget swimming in the crystal clear waters of Lake Erie and tanning our bodies on the best sand beaches in Canada. Plus, it was sheer heaven aboard the Crystal Beach Boat as it sailed to exciting ports.

How ironic that these wonderful memories ended in tragedy for me in 1966. At the end of a family outing, my seven-year-old daughter wanted just one more ride with her cousin as they were leaving the Park. The Airborne was a new ride, not properly tested for children and was the scene of this tragedy. She was thrown from the bottom of a "car" from a height of forty feet. She suffered life threatening injuries, brain damage and total amnesia. She spent three months in Buffalo's Children Hospital with five specialists. Those doctors along with much prayer saved her life. It was the most serious accident in Park history other than the deaths that occurred on the Cyclone and Backety Back roller coasters. None of our family visited the Park for the next twenty years.

When the Park was closed in 1989, we were left with bittersweet memories.

Air-Borne in action, May 28, 1966.
Courtesy of Buffalo State College, Courier Collection

"... money from heaven."

Robert Tripp

I lived in Ridgeway and walked to Crystal Beach with my friends as a kid. We enjoyed the open access to Crystal Beach Park in the 1960's. We would gather beneath the Roll-O- Planes because they gave us money from heaven. The gyrating action while twisting on their axis would jiggle the pockets of the patrons twirling above us. We scrambled for the coins and spent them on the HEYDEY, Wild Mouse and Giant coaster. It was a very sad day when Crystal Beach Park closed its gates.

Calypso — ready for the spring opener, May 19, 1967.
Courtesy of Buffalo State College, Courier Collection

"The Village," the community from the 60's TV series, "The Prisoner."

Gary Swiatowy

I went to St. Teresa's Catholic grade school in Akron N.Y. in the 60's. Annually we took a school field trip to Crystal Beach. Pretty much the whole school took a couple of buses up there for the day, with the nuns as chaperones. This meant that we were pretty much on our own.

I recall paying something like $10 for 100 tickets which could be used on both rides and food. That was more than enough to keep you busy for the day.

My favorites were the Magic Carpet, which had to be one of a kind. You had to squeeze through the "rollers" at the entrance. This and the carpet ride at the end were unique. In today's society the liability issues would prevent this.

I have never seen a fun house like that anywhere else, with the tilted room, the black lights, and the "air jets" when you least expected them. Laugh in the Dark was another of my favorites, as well as the bumper boats, and the antique cars.

Remember this was back in my elementary school days. I always looked forward to the waffles as well. We would spend the day and do it all including miniature golf. Only once though did I brave the Wild Mouse. Once was enough!

But let me point out some things I do not remember. I do not remember having to pay for parking. I also do not remember having to wait for more than a few minutes to get on any ride. I do not remember having to walk a half mile just to get to the entrance. And I do not remember anyone frisking me to make sure that I did not bring any food or beverage into the place.

This was a different time and a different era. Crystal Beach was a fun place, where 2 busloads of kids could be cut loose and found at the end of the day both safe and tired.

My parents also took my brother and myself there as well quite a few times. It was a fun family day trip that we could enjoy together and afford. Unlike the parks of today where you have to take out a second mortgage for a day in the park. Then return home more stressed out than anything else.

"You don't know what you've lost til it's gone" A couple of years ago, my wife and I were on our way to Welland and detoured just to look at the remains. We saw the "gated" community which replaced Crystal Beach Park. What immediately came to mind was "The Village", the community from the 60's TV series "The Prisoner". So these people got their private beach and a type of living they could have put anywhere else. We lost a piece of history while pockets got filled. I also noticed the rest of the town has become quite run down as there are no tourists to support the few businesses. This brought a tear to my eye. Crystal Beach can never be replaced, I wish it was still there as a place where I could entertain my grandchildren.

"... my memories would last a lifetime."

Tim Wagner

Crystal Beach has so many memories for me. Fortunately, as a filmmaker, I've had an opportunity to document that very special place in my heart. And even better, to share those visual memories with others.

As an amusement park and roller coaster enthusiast, I take my hobby seriously. Between 1981 and 1991, I shot over 5 hours of Super 8mm film at Crystal Beach. Though I only knew Crystal in its later days, the 1960s until the end. I have many memories from family and friends of the parks earlier days. And these collective memories include the Canadiana.

But there's so much more than the sights in the park. There are the unique sounds and smells as well. In 1984, I spent a day recording the sounds unique to Crystal Beach such as the air-jets at the Magic Palace, Laughing Sal,

**Whirling back against the cage wall, five Depew youngsters
enjoy the Roundup, July 26, 1977.**
Courtesy of Buffalo State College, Courier Collection

Charming Charlie and an on-board ride of Laff In The Dark. Plus, I saved the sounds of the Comet and Giant roller coasters, as well as the voice of Leo the Paper Eating Lion. What I couldn't capture were the smells that Crystal Beach had to offer such as cinnamon suckers, freshly made caramel corn, sugar waffles, bumper cars, Jungle Land, the HEYDEY and the roller coaster grease. How sad that we can't record such unique fragrances.

From my childhood, I remember my family's annual drive to the park and the butterflies in my stomach. Then came my smile and laughter at the first glimpse of the "yellow roller coaster" and the colourful spires of the Magic Carpet. Then there were the unique sounds of Jungle Land with the splashing waterwheel and the wailing figure who was dunked and dunked again; the wooden conveyor belts that brought the boats up out of the water; the sleek animal heads on the front of the boats and the wonder when the boat melted into a dark tunnel. I remember as well the buzzing chain drive of the Laff In The Dark cars and the endless spirals of track. And who can forget the non-stop laughter of Laughing Sal and the piano tunes of Charming Charlie.

There was the joy of putting trash into the gaping maw of Leo the Lion, with his endless appetite for paper plates and napkins, chewing gum wrappers and cigarette butts. There was the smell of the HEYDEY as I rode the bumper boats next door. Then there was the rumbling sound of the HEYDEY cars and the dizzying whirl in the back corner if the car hit it just right.

I remember the tight turns of the Wild Mouse and the seat-bounce on those dips! There was the fear and exhilaration of my first ride on the Comet that was followed by a delicious Sugar Waffle. I was anxious as we left the park for dinner at Teal's hotel with aunts, uncles and grandparents. Then there was the sadness as we left the park at night. I stared out the back window of our car, not wanting to lose sight of such a magical place, knowing it would be a whole year before I'd return.

As an adult, I visited Crystal Beach weekly in the summer. We stood outside the Caramel Corn stand and savoured the heavenly aroma. We even helped Sam break in the Comet before the park opened. I met and befriended employees such as Shirley and Lucy at the sucker stand and Brad and Brian who made the suckers and the kisses. As well, Helen shared her stories of making Caramel Corn and Candy Apples. And Scotty gave us a tour through the Laff In The Dark. I also spent countless hours on the Comet, filming every angle.

I remember when the Crystal Ballroom opened again and boat service returned to the park. There were also many coaster-club events at Crystal Beach with delightful mid-summer exclusive rides on the Comet. I treasured those moments in the last several years, knowing the park would someday close forever.

And then it happened. On the final morning, I stood outside the Giant Coaster with Norm, enjoying the calm before the crowds came for the last time. That's when I knew my memories would last a lifetime.

"I REMEMBER CRYSTAL BEACH"

Stereo DVD or VHS Videotape – 67 minutes, $20.95 US, plus shipping.

"THE Canadiana & CRYSTAL BEACH"

Stereo DVD or VHS Videotape – 58 minutes, $20.95 US, plus shipping.

"SOUNDS OF CRYSTAL BEACH"

Stereo Audio Cassette – 30 minutes, $8.95 US, plus shipping

To order, or for more information, contact: Tim Wagner at (585) 425-7072 or rwagner@rochester.rr.com

Texas Revolver, June 5, 1977. Van Hall, hands on hips, impressed with ride that whisks passengers in a 360 degree loop.
Courtesy of Buffalo State College, Courier Collection

"... the Crystal Beach Boat"

Ed Cuddihy, Buffalo News

She was a queen, but they called her a boat, never a ship. Sure parents said she had a name, the S. S. Canadiana they called her, but to the kids on the block, she was just the Crystal Beach Boat.

Some days in the summer everyone on the Kensington trolley would be going down to board her. The walk from Main Street down to the end of Commercial Street where she was docked seemed to take forever when your legs were small. You passed the popcorn man and the man with a million balloons. You saw the old wooden huts, one opened in front to make a seafood stand, clams maybe, but most of the people had their own lunches in baskets. You went through a short tunnel and there she was. You could see her now, white and shiny and big. Some people said they painted her every year to hold her together. You enter the building under the big sign, "ENTRANCE TO STEAMERS" to the waiting room and ticket window. This was the room with wire screens that kept you confined there until the people got off the boat and it was made ready for the return trip to Crystal Beach.

You waited in line for tickets if you hadn't already bought them at the little stand at Kensington and Bailey. You counted your copper and steel pennies, shuffled your feet and anxiously waited. They finally open the screen to let you and your fellow voyagers out into the sunlight again. It was a magical place to be among the giant hawsers and pilings, traversing the ominous looking water surging below as you crossed the gang plank, moving with the motion of the ship. It was an experience that added to your life way beyond the excitement of the moment.

Three thousand, they used to say. That's how many could get on her at one time. What was not well known is that often, an excess of four thousand people were loaded onto the boat at the end of the day. People walked uphill over the gangplank to get on the boat to the beach. Everyone had their day of fun in the sun and waited for the last boat to go home. When you got back to the dock in Buffalo, you walked uphill again to get off the boat. It was not that the dock got higher.

Those trips began with the traditional blasts which told the last people at the ticket window to hurry. You found a spot on the rail and looked at the city hall clock and the old cathedral. A final blast and you were off. The sights of the waterfront kept you spellbound as you sailed past the towering black erector set of track and structures where they dumped coal into railroad cars. Then you swung around, past the lighthouse and glided into the open lake.

Now the queen swayed and you hoped you wouldn't get seasick like before. Inside, some kids bought popcorn and peanuts in their shells, but not you. You plugged your nickel into a machine that promised a wristwatch if you were skilful enough to draw a claw crane, but most of the time, it delivered nothing. If you tired of that, it was always fun to try and print your name on an aluminum good luck charm that had a penny in the center. This was a machine that pressed letters into the metal and you had to be very careful or you would make a mistake and mess it all up. The usual results were three bad ones for every one that was almost right.

Outside, you sat on one of the park benches on the open deck and watched the Canadian shore. You watched the waves the boat made and the great churning wake. You watched, fascinated by the engine that was so big and powerful. The 75 minute ride would have been too short if the beach wasn't waiting. Still to come was the first glimpse of the roller coaster, the rides on the Caterpillar and the powdered waffles bought from the lady in the pink uniform.

Laughter was subdued on the return trip. Everyone was tired, a little dizzy maybe, almost wishing the day was over, but not wanting it to end.

The city looked big over the breakwater. Then they tied up the queen and opened the gates. Fathers carried the little kids, mothers dragged the others, up the hill toward the Terrace, Main Street and the trolley. You could look back and see the Canadiana's lights like a symbol of happiness on the waterfront.

Times would change and many years would go by before you'd ask, "I wonder what every happened to the Crystal Beach Boat and I wonder why?"

Crystal Beach Park Fatalities
Scenic Railway Death-1910

Seventeen-year-old Louise Koch from Orchard Park N.Y. was killed in June of 1910 while riding the scenic railway at Crystal Beach Park. She sat alone in a seat behind two friends and as the train rounded a bend a human shriek frightened her friends. Louise Koch was not in her seat. Searchers found her body between the tracks. She was returned to Buffalo aboard the ferry Americana. Louise died soon after the boat left for Buffalo. This ride was known as the Backety Back Scenic Railway roller coaster and had a twister layout, not to be confused with the tame and gentle Miniature Railway.

Cyclone Fatality-1938

The nurse on duty at the Cyclone roller coaster could not help 22-year-old Amos Wiedrich of Black Rock N.Y. on May 20, 1938.

While the Cyclone climbed its first hill, Amos stood up and tried to remove his jacket. Sadly his arms got stuck in the jacket behind his back and he was thrown from his seat on the first drop of the coaster. His body landed on a lower track and he was run over by his own coaster. His body was dragged for 200 feet.

At the trial for damages launched by his family, Wiedrich's coaster companion claimed that the safety bar came open at the top of the incline. Weidrich's family was awarded $3000 in damages.

Comet Coaster Fatality-1975

Kieran Glynn of Stevensville was killed in 1975 when thrown from the last car of the Comet as it swirled around a bend at nearly 60 miles per hour. Officials said that this was the only fatality on the Comet since its debut in 1948. During this period, 1948-1975, officials claimed that nine million people had enjoyed a ride on the Comet.

"And on the way back, we always had to stop at a deli and buy that delicious Canadian Loganberry, chocolate milk, and Canadian bacon for breakfast."

Cinnamon in Oregon

The Merry-Go-Round with that big stationary lion and the big boxes along the outside? The Merry-Go-Round was right next to Leo the Paper Eating Lion. Loved Leo with his scratchy voice!

The Tumblebug... And yep, still remember the old Caterpillar. The bumper boats that you drove. Remember the big long hook that the operator used to bring the boats in?

Let Junior Take the Family for a Ride? And yes...I do remember that awful cauldron with the human skull and the big old grin on the person's face at the Jungle Land. And Charming Charlie and Laughing Sal at the Laff In the Dark. And the Wax Museum downstairs.

Ken-Bailey Days! Bells IGA used to give out free ride tickets for A's and B's on report cards. And we'd all board the bus at the corner of Kensington and Bailey Aves and ride down there.

116

Oh the memories! I can still see my mom, dad, brothers, sisters, aunt, uncle, cousins, great-aunts, and Gramps - even some gal pals from high school- all bunched around a huge picnic table in the picnic grove between Kiddie Land and the Yellow Coaster, spreading cold-cuts and mustard on sandwiches, and drinking Loganberry and Canadian chocolate milk! Do you still remember all the yellow jacket bees that hung around the picnic tables?

The HeyDey was a group ride for us. Our extended family filled up 2 or 3 entire cars. Think the HeyDay was my favorite. But then again...maybe the Scrambler was. The Ferris Wheel, the Flume.

Still remember my first rides on both the Yellow Giant Coaster and the Comet. I was a very timid child - but my older cousin took me under her wing and sat beside me and instructed me in the fine art of screaming as you went down the first hill. The Comet was awesome next to the Lake!

Frozen custard! Ummmmmm-mmmmm-mmmmm.

Ohhh, ohhhh! Remember near the Wild Mouse, you'd go up these steps to this raised garden with benches? I can still see my great-aunts sitting up there in their flowery dresses, silk hose, and handbags waiting for us.

And that beach! Again, an entire extended family affair. My aunt would bring this huge inflatable raft and we'd all ride on it. Our family had a styrofoam 2 seater. And the slope was so gradual - you could walk WAY out. And there was that big diving and sunbathing raft out aways. And remember that bathing house where you got changed? How damp it always was?

And our last ride of the evening was always an entire family ride on the train that went around back of the cottages. Even got Gramps and the great-aunts on that one!

And on the way back to Buffalo, we always had to stop at a deli and buy that delicious Canadian Loganberry, chocolate milk, and Canadian bacon for breakfast. And then we usually did a "naughty". We bought illegal fireworks at one of the stands and snuck them past Customs at the Peace Bridge. Whoops! Blush....don't think the Lord would want me doing that today.

Last time I visited my family back in Buffalo, we drove out there to see what it looked like - and I almost cried. It was all a big court of new homes! But we still found the old parking lot just outside the old entrance. It still had some of the old fencing. This brought tears to my eyes.

Ready to Zip. A new ride opened with the Crystal Beach season on Memorial Day called the Zipper - May 18, 1973.

Courtesy Buffalo State College, Courier Collection

Play Area in Merger, May 24, 1969

– Courier Express

The play area for Western New York and Southern Ontario is Crystal Beach Amusement Park. It is in the process of merging with the Recreation Corp. of America, the $3 million transaction to be completed in late June or July. Stockholders of Crystal Beach Transit Company Inc., which operates the amusement area, will receive debentures from the Florida based Recreation Corp. of America.

"My favourite ride, the Wild Mouse."

John, Las Vegas, Nevada

So many memories have come back to me. I grew up in Niagara Falls, New York and as a kid it was a big event to go to Crystal Beach. As I got older, I would rent a cottage every year and use it several times a week. I moved away in the early 70's and never again got the chance to get back there. I will always remember those wonderful summers spent at the Beach, and especially my favourite ride, the Wild Mouse.

"My house was a party-house..."

Barbara Levy Cantor

I left Buffalo in 1985 but not a day goes by when I don't think about Crystal Beach and the magic that it gave to my life. I long for the day when I can return and see it one more time.

I was brought there as an infant and lived in my papa and grandparents' cottage, David and Kathryn Unherr. They bought their cottage in 1928 and moved it from Derby Road to West Lincoln where it still remains.

My childhood summers were all spent at Crystal Beach. We moved to our own cottage at 7 Cherrywood when I was seven. My house was a party house. My parents allowed me to have parties with blaring music, gangs of kids as friends, many from Toronto. We danced at the Swing Inn, drove down the main road in convertibles to show off that we were here, went to Jacks for French fries and then kibbutzed at the stand. Of course we went to the park for waffles, suckers and then had someone read our fortunes. We always tried to sneak into the beach and this mean old lady tried to keep us out.

It was the most fantastic existence that a child and teenager could ever have. When they had the talent shows, I remember carrying my sister Jackie there to sing with Richie Goldstein and Irwin Sandler. My closest friends Marsha Miller, Linda Siegleman, Rochelle Bentovitch and Annette Lipman and many more, all have the same memories.

And oh, what about those rainy days when we watched the Doris Day, Gene Kelly and Fred Astair movies?

In 1978, my dream was to come back to Crystal Beach and I bought my own cottage at the top of the hill on Cherrywood. I was able to raise my own children there for 8 years-Jennifer, Jacob and Rosie. Although they didn't have the same experience as I did, they did get a taste of what it was like to live in magical Crystal Beach. It will always remain a special place in my heart.

Remembering Crystal Beach

Margaret Franklin

Back in the summer of 1977, my dad took me to Crystal Beach for the first time! It was a wonderful place! Best of all was the fact that you could pay one price to get in and go on as many rides as you wanted to, as many times as you wanted! That was the first time I'd ever seen a "Pay-One-Price" park.

So, of course I headed straight for the carousel. I love carousels in general and this was one of my favorites, P.T.C# 12, perhaps the penultimate menagerie carousel built by the Philadelphia Toboggan Company. After 1918, they stopped building menagerie carousels and concentrated strictly on all horses. Anyway, I remember this carousel being one of the coolest things I'd ever seen. Despite its art-deco renovations with multicolored duct-tape wound around the poles and layers of garish park paint, PTC #12 had some of the most exquisite carvings I've ever seen!

My favorite was the hippocampus, a mythical creature that was half horse and half fish. It had a swirling green tail and a saddle that consisted of a lily-pad adorned with a conch shell and a lobster.

Other animals included a big St. Bernard dog with its famous brandy barrel around its neck, a pair of leaping leopards, deer, goats, a camel, giraffe lion and tiger as well as a couple donkeys. There was also a rare, one-of-a-kind PTC wolf, although with all that garish park paint, it looked more like a border collie! I think during the course of the day I rode examples of every menagerie creature that was there plus several different horses. My favorite horse was a standing white stargazer with blue and lilac trappings.

120

Nina Schaefer and Bruce Bell of Clarence enjoy kids
in a sand sculpture contest, August 8, 1982.
Courtesy of Buffalo State College, Courier Collection

121

Another highlight of the day was going on the Comet. It was the best roller-coaster ever! My dad and I rode right in the very front seat with a dizzying view of Lake Erie to our right!

In the summers to follow my dad would usually drive my friends and I to Crystal Beach to celebrate birthday parties. It was always an enjoyable fun-filled day, complete with our favorite rides and good food! Crystal Beach was famous for its "Elephant Ears" which were oversized Danish pastries with various fruit toppings. Then there were the "Sugar Puffs", a crunchy, deep-fried daisy-shaped biscuit dipped in powdered sugar. Crystal Beach was also the first place I ever had one of those giant hot pretzels with mustard. There was also their logan berry juice and the best chocolate milkshakes I'd ever had that were so thick you could barely get them through the straw! And of course no visit was complete without bringing home a bag of their famous salt-water taffy! It was a variety of flavors in multicolored wrappers. Now we buy similar stuff at Niagara Falls, but that's another story.

Last time I was at Crystal Beach, in 1989, their last season of being open to the public, I was absolutely heartbroken to discover that my beloved PTC#12 was gone! In its place, not far from its original location was a rather nice 1950's aluminum carousel, but it could never put a candle to those precious menagerie figures! I could barely bring myself to ride it but I went on anyway. It was nice, but it just wasn't the same. And the pavilion that used to house PTC #12 now held a variety of midway games.

Perhaps I had been in denial, because before I went there, PTC#12 was not listed in the census at the back of my "Painted Ponies" book. In fact, there is a picture of my beloved hippocampus being stripped of his park paint, but I ceased to make the connection. Could it really be him in that picture? Indeed it was, and although he now belongs to a private collector, I am happy to say I've seen him in recent years on the cover of an issue of "Carousel News and Trader", restored and looking better than ever!

Carousels have always been a major fascination of mine. Besides PTC #12 at Crystal Beach, another childhood favorite of mine is the classic Dentzel Menagerie at Centre Island in Toronto. I am happy to say it still exists despite plans to auction it off in 1988. The public fought to keep this treasure!

I am also happy to say that the Kremers Illions/Looff menagerie at Port Dalhousie still runs every summer charging its original price of only a nickel a ride! I recently celebrated my 40th birthday there and had a wonderful time.

Paramount Canada's Wonderland has yet another classic Philadelphia Toboggan Company carousel, P.T.C#84, which previously operated at Palisades Park in New Jersey. My good friend Richard Concepcion (who by the way is one of the few people who knows more about carousels than I do) has the opportunity to ride it in both locations!

Another local treasure I've been to is the 1906 CW Parker carousel in Roseneath, Ontario. It was closed to the public for several years, but re-opened beautifully restored with the horses adopted by local sponsors on July 17th, 1993.

The North Bay carousel opened in July of 2002, a Hershell-Spillman frame repopulated with horses created by local artists and adopted by various sponsors.

The Guelph carousel, built by Herschell-Spillman was restored in the early 80's by artist Ken Danby, more renowned for his hockey paintings.

The carousel at Woodbine Centre in Etobicoke, Ontario consists of the original Looff mechanism from Redondo Beach, California, repopulated with modern fiberglass horses by Bradley & Kaye who were in more recent years bought out by Chance Amusements. This carousel has some lovely replicas of various artists' horses including Illions and Parker. My particular favorite is a palomino PTC stander adorned with a pair of kissing cherubs.

I have been a member of the National Carousel Association for a number of years on and off and traveled extensively visiting various carousels in Canada and the U.S. Someday I would like to write a book about all the carousels I've been to, especially the ones here in Ontario.

Carousels are the main subject of most of my artistic creations. You can visit my website at http://margaretfranklin.netfirms.com

The Merry-Go-Round.
Harvey Holzworth Collection

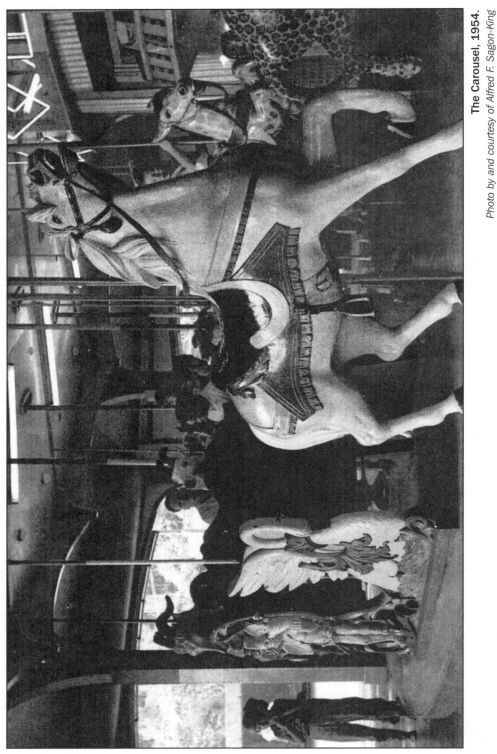

The Carousel, 1954.

Photo by and courtesy of Alfred F. Sagon-King

Fun In The Park

– Courier Express, May 28, 1977

Closing tonight is 11 o'clock. Sunday hours are 1:30 to 11 p.m. and Memorial Day hours are 12:30 to 11 p.m. General admission includes all rides except the Comet and the Texas Revolver.

No Money Premium

– Courier Express, August 18, 1979

The television often suggests that you "come to Crystal Beach," a 30 minute drive across the border. Should you take its advice, you will find a menu that ranges from 75-cent frankfurters to $3.25 chicken and chips dinners. You will pay $6.25 to go on all the rides you want if you're an adult; $4.25 if you are under 12; nothing if you are under four. And you will receive no exchange on your American money.

But you will find a large, neatly-maintained area of rides for children, including a Merry-Go-Round that goes around and around so many times that people yell, "Stop it already." Crystal Beach has spook houses, a sky lift, a roller coaster inside a Ferris wheel that literally hangs its riders upside down-and the Comet.

"...I was called to the riots."

Bob Long

I hung around the Crystal Beach area all my life. I was married in 1959 and prior to that my wife and I enjoyed many big bands that came to the Crystal Beach Ballroom. Between band sets, we'd leave the ballroom and ride the roller coaster.

In 1965, I joined the police force in Bertie Township. At that time, the Ontario Provincial Police patrolled Crystal Beach. I had played drums with the Bob Carpenter orchestra and other groups, but as a policeman back then you could not have a second job. That's why I was afraid to take any jobs playing drums until about 1970. Then I got a call to go to the Palmwood in Crystal Beach and play drums in a band. Prior to that, I played at a place on the corner of Erie and Ridgeway Road. I played with the top musicians including Janice Joplin's organ player. That place was packed with patrons who lined up to get in every Friday and Saturday night until Labour Day.

Can-Am Swing Band.
ERNO ROSSI

After that you could fire a gun across the room and not hit anybody.

While I was working on the Bertie police force, I was called to Crystal Beach to help with the traffic during the riots. I remember the Ontario Hotel on the corner where they used to drink and fight it out on the street. There was so much traffic that I would have to walk to a police call because the streets were jammed with cars.

In 1983, I almost got killed in an accident with the police cruiser and I was laid up for a long time. It was 1987 when I got a call from Bob Carpenter about bringing the bands back into the Crystal Beach Ballroom. That's how I got back into playing drums. I played the ballroom for two nights to wall-to-wall people.

Rick Doan, Paul Kassay, Janet Truckenbrodt and Bob Steckley decided to have a memorabilia day for Crystal Beach. They asked me to put the music end of it together. I formed a band called the Can-Am-Big Band consisting of a majority of people from Buffalo who had worked over the years at the Crystal Beach Ballroom. Several of the guys had played with the Glenn Miller and Tommy Dorsey bands. We put the band together and it still plays great music today. The Can-Am Swing Band is a smaller version and continues to entertain many people.

There was an amazing bury the summer parade on Labor Day weekend when they would carry a casket (summer) from Bay Beach down Erie Road to the Palmwood Hotel. That was one big party the whole weekend.

Roll-O-Plane — spring service, May 19, 1972.
Courtesy of Buffalo State College, Courier Collection

Preserving A Part Of Our Past

By George Kunz—- Oct. 30/84 Courtesy Buffalo News

The Canadiana is the stuff that dreams are made of. As a boy, I ran along the ship's decks clutching my Buffalo Evening News Amusement Coupons. I watched the mighty engines as they churned up the rancid waters of Buffalo Harbor for another trip to Crystal Beach. My head was teeming with visions of the Caterpillar, HEYDEY, Tumblebug and Hall's cinnamon suckers.

When I was a young man, I escorted summer girl friends across the Canadiana's gangplank. Now my dreams focused on the Cyclone, the dance hall and naturally the long, late, boat-ride home. The Canadiana meant romance.

One chilly summer afternoon in 1965, I thought that I had paid the good ship my final farewell. I had read of the ship's hapless adventures after it left Buffalo—how it had been transferred to Toledo, had suffered a smashed nose in an accident, been towed back to Buffalo, and all but given up for dead. Moored at the foot of Amherst Street for years, the Canadiana slowly sank into ignominious decline.

Then I read with sorrow that the ship was to be pulled to Cleveland for a final disposition, and I knew that it was time for my last melancholy goodbye

The Pirate spring test run, May 21, 1980.
Courtesy of Buffalo State College, Courier Collection

128

to an old friend. Leaving my wife in charge of Child #3, I took the two older children with me to see the Canadiana.

The old ship seemed ashamed to see me. Like a once-proud lady fallen on bad times, the Canadiana listed. Its paint was blistered, windows were broken, and posts were rusting. My two-year old daughter began to cry.

I tried to explain to my children that this was authentic Buffalo history. Holding my son by the hand, I carried Mary, still howling, along the decks, through the paneled sitting room, across the dance floor, up the ladder to the third deck.

That afternoon there was broken glass everywhere; abandonment and decay hung in the air. It took real imagination to think of this as the Canadiana, the stuff of dreams. Haunted by ghosts of happier times, I paid my final farewell.

Final farewell? Maybe not. A courageous group, called The Friends of the Canadiana, is trying to bring the old legend back to Buffalo—where it belongs. The hope is to tow the ship back from its present berth in Ashtabula, and then gradually restore it.

What a terrific idea! The Canadiana, like Shea's Buffalo or the Wilcox Mansion, is a window to yesterday. Future generations can clasp hands with the past on its decks. High point of summer for children of my depression era was the ride to Crystal Beach on the Canadiana, and I'll bet half the married couples in Western New York shared that late boat trip together on Saturday nights.

Such a dream of restoring the Crystal Beach boat is costly, and there is a fund-raising party at the Hyatt Regency tonight to help the dream get afloat. I will be there with my whole family, hoping to meet old girl friends of fondly remembered moonlight cruises. One of these girl friends is coming along, because if she didn't, I'd divorce her.

"...the Buffalo Sabres hockey team."

Jim Poltrone, Dayton, Ohio

I made several trips to Crystal Beach while growing up in the Buffalo area. My last trip there was to see Larry Gowen in concert at the Crystal Ballroom in 1988.

I also remember the TV commercial featuring members of the Buffalo Sabres hockey team-one saying, "Forwards!" the other saying, "Backwards!" This was right after the park reversed one of the cars, so that people could ride the Comet facing backwards. At the end of the commercial were both players, in uniform, walking away from the camera...with wet seats.

Competition for Crystal Beach

Owners Joseph Biondolillo, Ed Hall and Rudy Bonifascio blamed the1989 closing of the park on the competition from new theme parks. Fantasy Island on Grand Island, N.Y., Darien Lake Park in Darien Center, N.Y., Canada's Wonderland near Toronto, and Marineland in Niagara Falls, Ontario all were in competition with Crystal Beach Amusement Park.

Folk hero Paul Bunyan is swarmed by Kenmore cuties. From left are Jenny Meyer-10, Mary Hall-11, Lisa Armstrong-13 and Tracey Hall-13 on July 1, 1981.
Courtesy of Buffalo State College, Courier Collection

ENJOY THE LAKE

ON

3 HOUR LAKE RIDE

OPTIONAL STOPOVER IN BUFFALO!

EVERY DAY EXCEPT MONDAY

LEAVES CRYSTAL BEACH PARK
12:00 & 3:40 P.M.

LEAVES BUFFALO
2:00 & 5:30 P.M.

TICKETS

Derby (Golf Course) Entrance To Park

ADULTS: $14.75   CHILDREN: $7.50

(ONE WAY TICKETS ARE HALF PRICE)

1988

Crystal cool in a heat wave.
Courtesy of Buffalo State College, Courier Collection

"...as the perfect suckers came out of the machine."

Bob Steckley

I grew up in Ridgeway, Ontario, Canada. My first memories of The Crystal Beach Park were from my father's annual company picnic at the park. We would start the day over at the stadium and play different games like ball toss, and three legged races. Then we would go to the park for a great picnic lunch. The afternoon and evening were spent riding the rides and enjoying all that Crystal Beach had to offer. We looked forward to that company picnic all year long!

I was about 7 years old when my father first took me on the Comet. I was about 6 inches too short when I stood up to the wooden cut-out of a child. The attendant told my father that I was too small. My father said, "He's going on now. Get out of my way!" Surprisingly the guy did allow me to go on.

I was terrified as the Comet clanked its way up to the top of the first hill. I was even more terrified when it went screaming down that first amazing drop. I think I screamed the whole way through that first ride. At the end of the ride, my legs were shaking and I could hardly speak, but I was hooked for life. The Comet was my favorite ride for many more years to come.

In the year 2002, I took my wife and two children aged 8 and 9 at the time, down to Great Escape Park in Lake George, NY to ride the comet again. My daughter is a daredevil and was really looking forward to the ride after hearing me talk about it so much. My son is not so adventurous and was probably shaking about as much as I was when I first rode it. They both loved it and we went on it many more times that day. I am glad that my kids were able to experience a little bit of my youth.

Living so close to Crystal Beach as a child meant that we got to go there many times each summer. My parents would drop my brothers and me off for a couple of hours in the evening. We only had a couple of dollars and it always seemed to disappear so fast. I used to stand near the exit and ask people if they had any tickets left over. I put my saddest face on and usually got enough tickets to keep busy for another hour or so.

One of our favorite things to do was to stop our boat in the jungle boat ride. We would hold the boat against the sides and sit very quietly until the boat behind us would run into ours. Right at that moment we would all scream as loud as we could to throw an even bigger scare into the unsuspecting people behind us.

The Wild Mouse was another scary ride. I think it was so scary because the cars were just out in the open on this little track. It seemed like you were going to go right over the edge.

As we got older, Crystal Beach became the prime spot to look for girls. I think every guy within 100 miles of CB went cruising there at one time or another. Once the park started to charge admission instead of free admission, we only went a couple of times a year.

I was born in 1960 so I never got the chance to ride the Canadiana. I have heard many stories from customers over the years about how great it was.

In 1985 I worked at the park as one of the food managers. It was my job to mix up the sugar waffle batter for the day. They kept the recipe pretty secret and only myself and one other guy knew it that year.

That recipe came in handy in 1993. I owned a small restaurant in Ridgeway. I started to make the sugar waffles as a dessert item. Before long I had customers coming from Buffalo and even Hamilton to buy the waffles. That's why I booked a hundred dollar space at an area craft show to sell the waffles.

In preparation for the show I cooked 700 waffles, one at a time. That morning it was raining pretty heavily and it wasn't supposed to stop all day. I had to work the restaurant that day, so my wife and my friend ran the booth at the craft show. My wife was furious at me for "wasting one hundred dollars and she said that we would be eating waffles for a long time. Around noon the phone rang at the restaurant and it was my wife. She said, "We are out of waffles. What should I do?" I said, "Apologize to me and keep cooking as fast as you can".

Within the year, I had sold the restaurant and started the Crystal Beach Candy Company. We had a trailer built and started doing shows every weekend in the summer months. The reaction to our product was amazing. We trademarked the name, The Original Crystal Beach Sugar Waffle. Our unique red trailer became a crowd favorite at each of the 30 shows we do each year.

Around 1995 I called Bob Hall down in Ft. Lauderdale to see if he would sell me the sucker making equipment and recipes for the Hall's Original Suckers. He said he wasn't ready to sell it yet because it had been in the family for too long. It was in storage and wasn't being used but he couldn't bring himself to sell it. I continued to call him twice a year, but I always got turned down.

Then in February of 2001 I called again. This time Bob said, "You sure are persistent about this. I think we need to meet face to face". My uncle and I flew down to Florida in March to meet with Bob Hall. Bob had a candy business in Florida and was too busy to take time off to meet us so we went

Brian Gray, 9, son of Mr. and Mrs. George R. Gray of Cheektowaga, is not amused at Crystal Beach Amusement Park, when Marjorie Kopinski of Lockport takes a picture of Brian under Paul Bunyan.

Courtesy of Buffalo State College, Courier Collection

and worked at his shop with him. He was pretty standoffish at first as he tried to get to know us. By the end of our first day there he had warmed up and took us out to his favorite restaurant for all you can eat shrimp. At dinner he said that he was very impressed with what I had done with my business so far. He then said that he had decided it was time to sell the sucker equipment. I was so happy I could have screamed.

Over the next two days we agreed upon a price for the equipment, the recipes, and the use of the Hall name. He said that he was going to visit his daughter in Georgia for a month and we could come back in May to pick up the equipment. I said that it had taken him 7 years to agree to sell to me, and that I didn't want to wait that long to pick up the equipment. This was a Tuesday afternoon and we were flying home that night. Bob said he was leaving for Georgia at noon on Friday and as long as we were there before he left for Georgia that we could pick it up.

We arrived home early Wednesday morning and I went and arranged financing for the equipment and looked into the paperwork needed to bring the equipment back into Canada. Thursday morning my Uncle and I started on the drive to Florida. We drove straight through and arrived in Ft. Lauderdale at 9:00 Friday morning. We spent two hours with Bob loading all the pieces of the machine into my truck. By noon we were headed back to Canada.

It took us about a month to get the machine cleaned up and running. Bob Hall wasn't in the best of health at this time and told us that if the doctors didn't find out what was wrong with him he feared he would be dead by August. He offered to come to Canada to help us with the startup, but with his health concerns we decided to have him talk us through the first batch on the phone.

As the candy was cooking, Bob was telling me step by step what to do. I had a headset on and was working as we talked. Once the candy got to the right texture it was time to run it through the machine. I can't begin to describe the joy and pride I felt as I saw the first suckers coming out of the machine looking perfect. That first batch ran perfectly and Bob sounded as thrilled for us as I felt.

We had to run 7 days a week all summer long just to keep up with the demand for the suckers. Bob would call me at the shop at least once a week to see how things were going. We sent lots of suckers down to him for his approval, and always enjoyed hearing back from him.

The annual Crystal Beach Festival was scheduled for August 11 that year. I had talked Bob Hall into coming up from Florida that year to attend the festival. Bob called me the Monday before the festival to say that his daughter and him would be there Saturday morning. The Saturday came and went without any appearance from Bob. I tried calling and got no answer and assumed they had run into trouble on the trip. On Sunday I received a phone call from a mutual friend who informed me that Bob had passed away the day he was to leave.

I don't think that Bob's decision to sell the equipment to me that year was an accident. I had never met Bob before that year but he sure made an impact on me for the five months I knew him. If Bob hadn't sold the equipment when he did, I don't think it would have ever been found. He had it in 3 different storage units and all the parts would not have been identifiable to anyone but him.

When I was a child at Crystal Beach I loved to watch the suckers coming off of the production line. I remember thinking what a cool job it must be to make candy. The peanut suckers were my favorite and I never left the park without one.

We are into our fourth year of production and I still get goose bumps when I see the suckers coming off of my production line. I am proud to keep some of the Crystal Beach Park traditions alive!

If you would like to see actual sucker production videos and pictures check out our website: www.crystalbeachcandy.com

Thanks for letting me share some of my Crystal Beach memories with you.

Flying Scooters ready for passengers.
Photo by and courtesy of Alfred F. Sagon-King

Canadiana, 1910-1956.
Courtesy and copyright — Richard Connor

S.S. Canadiana Trivia

Infamous Buffalo Waterfront. The waterfront area where the Canadiana docked was a notorious, poverty stricken area that reached its peak in infamy around 1870-75 when the Erie Canal was in full swing. In 50 area buildings there were 75 saloons, a slum that saw daily murders and was known as the most dangerous place in the world, even worst than Shanghai, China.

At the nearby clean, Canadian beaches such as Crystal Beach, the concerts, sermons and lectures gave way to the 1890 formation of The Crystal Beach Company, formed by American entrepreneur, John Evangelist Rebstock and his investors. The park was expanded, more beach-front was purchased and the first pier was built out into the lake. A rush of visitors kept 17 ferry boats busy, starting with the Dove up to the State of New York.

Navel architect Frank Kirby was commissioned to design a bigger ferry boat and the Americana was launched in 1908. Business boomed and the Canadiana followed in 1910. She served the Buffalo to Crystal Beach run until 1956.

Canadiana Maiden Voyage, May 30, 1910

The Buffalo Times reported the next day; "On both the trip over and the return, the mechanism worked with satisfying regularity; not a screw nor a nut gave trouble. The steamer left the dock at the foot of Illinois Street at 2:40 p.m. and pushing her prow through all types of craft in the harbor, each giving off its own toot, shriek or wheeze, she received a bedlam of gratifying salutes from all sides. Bustling tugs and motorboats greeted her progress down the river enthusiastically and as she turned into the lake and headed for the Canadian shore, huge freighters paid her homage by deep-toned blasts. She put in at Crystal Beach one hour and twenty minutes later. Her sister ship, Americana, was leaving the Canadian side as the new steamer headed for the pier. Salutes filled the air for several minutes accompanied by a frantic waving of handkerchiefs. The guests were given an hour ashore, and the return trip was then made.

Her fittings are beautiful, the arrangements perfect, her seaworthiness unquestioned and the entire apportionment all that could be desired in an excursion steamer. Even the most timid may enjoy a ride on these steamers, which are absolutely safe. They are fitted out with automatic fire and man-overboard signal stations at various points so that the captains and engineers can be immediately notified in case of accident."

Canadiana Maiden Voyage Music

During the maiden voyage of the Canadiana in 1910, its orchestra played the Canadiana March, composed for the occasion by Irving Tallis. The lady passengers received a gift copy of the music as a souvenir of the trip.

Canadiana Flags

She sailed under the Lake Erie Excursion Co. flag from 1910 to 1924 — the Buffalo and Crystal Beach Corp. flag from 1924 to 1947 — and the Crystal Beach Transit Co. flag from 1947 to 1956.

Canadiana Entertainers

The 74th Regiment Orchestra entertained on the Canadiana in the early days. So too did Duke Ellington, Guy Lombardo, famous lyricist and composer Harold Arlen, Paul Whiteman, Eddie Duchin, Cab Calloway, Woody Herman and many more. Harold Austin was the leader of a local orchestra that played both the Canadiana and the Crystal Ballroom for many years.

Harold Arlen was Hyman Arlick's stage name and he and his band played on the Canadiana in the 1920's. The band members split $80 per week in wages plus a bonus of free suppers. A Buffalo native, Arlen went on to an outstanding career as a singer, piano player and arranger in New York City. He was famous for composing such tunes as, Stormy Weather, all the music for The Wizard of Oz, That Old Black Magic, It's Only A Paper Moon and many other famous pieces.

Arlen stood the band instruments in their holders when not in use. One band member reported that the captain tried to knock these instruments

Canadiana inner stairwell of red mahogany wood from Honduras. Ornately carved balustrades and fluted columns on the grand staircase are typical of the era when the Canadiana was built in 1910.

Courtesy of Buffalo State College, Courier Collection

down each night as he docked the Canadiana at its Buffalo destination. An extra heavy bump at the dock usually did the trick.

Child Overboard

In the 1930's a passenger on board the Canadiana had fun throwing coins on the deck to the delight of the kids who scrambled for the money. A boy bounced a girl overboard in the rush for coins. An alert deckhand followed her into the water and saved her life.

Suicide Attempt

A depressed young lady in the 1940's jumped overboard from the deck of the Canadiana. She was depressed over the loss of her boy friend in World War Two. An alert crewmember dived into the lake and rescued her.

Death of a Pilot

During World War Two, a British pilot flying in a Royal Canadian Airforce Harvard trainer plane was killed while buzzing the Canadiana. The ship's passengers and pilot waved their hands in greetings as the pilot lost control of the plane and crashed to his death into the lake.

Mahogany Wood

Lounges on board the Canadiana were built with the rich, deep-red mahogany wood from Honduras. Such wood was expensive, beautiful and served well for marine construction.

Hemp Rope

The tail shaft went through a six foot enclosed section, which was packed tight with greased hemp rope for the water-seal.

Canadiana Oilers

While the boat was in operation, oilers were constantly at work. When sailing, every moving piece of machinery on the ship had to be oiled or greased in thirty minutes, and then the process was repeated.

Canadiana Food Island

The food island was a rectangular enclosure with a narrow counter running along a series of windows around the food area while an overhanging canopy extended along the top of the windows. The windows could be raised or lowered and were closed at the dock. When the window was down there was a sign, CLOSED AT DOCK.

Canadiana Washrooms

Men used a long trough along the inside of an external wall of the ship, with small dividers out from the wall that gave some privacy to the five sections in the trough. The trough tilted slightly downward on one end, through a pipe to the lake below. Standard toilets lined the inside wall of the small room. The horseshoe shaped seat was held up and away from the bowl when not in use. But when in use, the toilet seat rested on the bowl and kept open the bottom of the bowl until the person stood up.

Canadiana Lounges

The mahogany lounges were luxurious. Three-dimensional ceilings of grape clusters and vines adorned these rooms.

Canadiana Change of Ownership

The Lake Erie Excursion Company ran the boat and the park until the economy caused their downfall in 1924. They were then bought out by local businessmen, George C. Hall, Charles A. Laube (of Old Spain fame) and Mr. Diebold. These three men formed the Buffalo and Crystal Beach Corporation and operation of the park and the ship was transferred. Laube's Midway Restaurant continued to operate at the park for years but as the bonds were being paid off, George was also buying out the other men and he had taken the park over completely by 1950.

World War Two Gasoline Rationing

Canadiana business boomed during the gas rationing of the war years. Everyone was working and had money. But limited gasoline supplies curtailed traveling, except on the street cars and the Canadiana. Memorial Day in 1943 saw record crowds on the ship and at Crystal Beach Park. The boat had to make an extra trip back to Buffalo that night in order to bring back all the patrons.

Japan Surrenders, August 15, 1945

Buffalo screeched, boomed, whistled and roared on August 15, 1945 as the Canadiana neared her dock. Japan had surrendered. World War Two was finished. V-J Day, victory over Japan was here. Passengers in celebration, lined up to pull the rope for the Canadiana whistle.

Canadiana Slot Machines

Passengers enjoyed playing the Canadiana nickel slot machines prior to 1950. But that was too much fun for the Buffalo police, who armed with sledgehammers, crushed the one-arm money-makers on the dock.

Crystal Beach sunbathing in 1910 and 1975.

Very Romantic - Don Stumpf

"Does anyone remember in the late forties and fifties the cutoff of the bar on the boat when it crossed the Canadian border on the lake? The drinking age was 18 in New York State and 21 in Ontario, Canada at that time. The Captain knew that there were few people on board who were 21 or over, so they just shut the bar down. I also remember the 3 hour Saturday night dances inside the breakwall in Buffalo harbor. Very romantic!

Crystal Beach Fireworks

When the Canadiana pulled away from the Crystal Beach dock for its final return to Buffalo on Labor Day evening, the boat would stop off shore and allow the passengers to enjoy a massive fireworks display set off from the top deck of the Crystal Beach pier. Summer was over.

" I picked up a zip-gun"
ERNO ROSSI

I swept the asphalt in Crystal Beach Park as an early summer job on Memorial Day, 1956. The Looper twirled beside me and the kids screamed with excitement as they stepped on the pedals and tried for a complete summersault. There was a clunk, clunk and clunk as something bounced out of this amusement ride and then plunked at my feet.

I picked up a zip-gun, a homemade handgun held together with tape. It was ready to fire if I pulled back and then release the elastic straps. There was a .22 caliber long-rifle bullet in the steel pipe that served as a barrel. I removed the cartridge, put it in my pocket and then tossed the gun into the garbage-pail on my dolly and continued to sweep the waste paper.

Soon a 12-year-old boy ran up to me and asked with an east Buffalo accent, "Deed you fine me gun?" I told him that I found his gun and gave it to the policeman over there by the Waffle stand. The kid looked with wide eyes and then melted into the crowd.

I swept beside the waffle-stand and heard a thud from behind me. Another boy, about fifteen years old was knocked to the ground. Two other kids kicked his body and face and screamed obscenities in an east Buffalo dialect. More gang members joined this brawl. Fists and feet flew in all directions. I faded backward with my back against the cafeteria wall, my paper-picking stick with the pointed end held tightly in my hands.

144

Then four white security men arrived waving long, thick clubs. They each grabbed a small, black spectator from behind and locked an arm around his neck. The security men used the little kids as a human shield and then cracked heads in the gang fight.

There was trouble all that day and also on the Crystal Beach Boat that ferried people back to Buffalo that night. As people crowded onto the dock that night, waiting for the return trip to Buffalo, explosions erupted among the passengers. The reckless use of fireworks such as M-80's, cherry bombs and firecrackers exploded in a free-fire war-zone among the crowd. People screamed in horror. And then lightning flashed on the open lake as the Crystal Beach Boat began to take on passengers.

The Canadiana finished that 1956 season and then was pulled for good from Crystal Beach service.

Buffalo Bills' AFL 1964 Championship Football Ring
Buffalo Bills' — 20   San Diego Chargers — 7

Paul Hudson, Port Colborne, Ontario, Canada.

We started scuba diving for coins beside the Crystal Beach dock in 1987- 88. At that time we used the new underwater metal detectors that had just come on the market. These new models came with earphones that pinged when the detector passed over buried coins. And did we hit a treasure trove!

Passengers on the Americana, Canadiana and other ferries used to throw coins overboard to the kids who were swimming near where the boats docked. Kids collected the coins from the sand bottom and then enjoyed a day in the park, compliments of the boat passengers.

The kids missed a lot of the coins that got covered with sand over the course of 100 years. And in our first 1987 scuba dive there, my partner and I collected about one coin per minute. In 20 dives that summer we picked up a total of 1500 coins. We also found 23 gold and silver rings, 3 gold chains, one ring with four diamonds in it and one 18 carat gold chain with a serpentine twist valued at $1000 dollars.

Among the coins there were Wheat Leaf pennies, Liberty nickels, Buffalo nickels, Mercury dimes, Liberty quarters and Walking Liberty half dollars. Most of the coins were American except for an 1844 coin issued by The Bank of Montreal called a bank token.

One of my most interesting finds was a very heavy Buffalo Bills 1964 AFL championship football ring containing 26 grams of gold. Inscribed in it was the score of that final game, Buffalo Bills - 20, San Diego Chargers -7, followed by the name Burr. I discovered that Burr was the Bills' assistant general manager and public relations director who had lost the ring in 1970. He was ecstatic when I returned it to him 17 years after he lost it.

I also returned another gold ring from the University of Virginia to its owner, William F. Cuddihy, a retired electrical engineer. He had worked for NASA and was instrumental in the 1976 Viking project that placed a probe on Mars. He was living in Yorktown Virginia, on Chesapeake Bay. He too was ecstatic when I returned his ring to him, 35 years after he lost it.

Canadiana Crew Sue For Back Wages
August 8, 1958

The 35 crew members of the Canadiana have asked the U.S. District Court in Toledo for government seizure of the vessel under admiralty law. The crew claim that the Seaway Excursion Lines Inc. of Detroit has not paid them their $28,000 in wages since July 16.

The Canadiana is owned by the Crystal Beach Transit Co. which charters the ship to Seaway Excursion Lines for $2500 a month. But Seaway Excursion Lines is behind in charter payments as well. Admiralty law says that the ship could be seized and sold for back wages.

On July 30, 1958 the ship was damaged when a bridge was closed on her steel hull. A shipyard strike held up repairs and the Seaway Co. ordered the crew to sign off the ship. But the crew argued that they have to stay aboard because the ship is stocked with food and they have no money to eat elsewhere.

"... Canadiana involved in a crash with a bridge."
ERNO ROSSI

The Canadiana was leased in 1958 to the Seaway Excursion Lines of Detroit for use between Toledo, Ohio and the Bob-Lo Island Amusement Park in the Detroit River. During one of her excursions with 885 passengers, the Canadiana crashed into a bridge that had carelessly been lowered in front of her. She was unable to stop her forward momentum. Consequently, the second and third bow-decks were badly damaged as steel screeched against steel sending the passengers into a panic to grab life jackets and to round-up kids and other loved ones. There were few injuries. But the Canadiana was again out of business.

An old dejected Canadiana returned to Buffalo in 1962. It sat neglected until 1966 and then was towed to Fairport, Ohio near Cleveland. Her ownership passed from hand to hand and port to port, as the good ship sank into the mud of the Cuyahoga River. This same river was once so polluted that it caught fire.

The Crystal Beach Boat was refloated in 1983, was towed and then sank again into the mud of the Ashtabula, Ohio harbor. She was raised again and was towed back to Buffalo where it again sank into the mud of the Buffalo harbor. Again refloated in 1988, she was towed to Port Colborne, Ontario, Canada where she found her final resting place—settled part way into the mud of a quiet cove in the Welland Canal.

Her funeral was in 2004 as cutting torches cremated her final remains at 94 years of age. I gave her a simple farewell for all who loved her. At her cremation, I gave thanks for all the happiness that she gave to me and to millions of people. Then I said goodbye for all of us. May she rest in peace.

For those of you who would like to see the summary of the four million, three hundred thousand dollar estimated restoration costs for the Canadiana, I've included the following:

Engineering Study (Abstract)

Marine Consultants & Designers (Canada) Ltd.

Mr. David Munro; Naval Architect

CANADIANA when hit by a bridge.
Cathy Herbert Collection

COMMENT - It is realized that the Canadiana has historic importance and at all times the historical integrity and maintenance of the original equipment and material has been kept in mind. However, since the intent is to operate the Canadiana as a passenger-carrying vessel, it must be treated by the United States coast Guard as a NEW vessel. As such, it must comply with all current regulations which are considerably more stringent now than when the Canadiana was built, particularly in the areas of passenger safety. Wooden construction is not acceptable so that the entire superstructure must be replaced with aluminum. Aluminum has the added advantage of being light and beneficial to stability which in turn allows more passengers to be carried. It can also be reproduced in textures which will duplicate the appearance of wood. All existing steel structural support pillars and girders will be retained. Wherever possible, the original wood paneling and moldings will be re-installed.

The Canadiana is a significant historic vessel for Buffalo. Its rehabilitation would be an asset in the waterfront development of the city. The fact that modern regulations have altered some of the construction details and materials, should not detract from its historical and commercial

Canadiana in 2004 awaits cremation in Port Colborne, Ontario.
Courtesy and copyright of artist, Richard Connor

attractiveness to Government agencies and the general public alike.

The cost estimate using current (August 1986) day prices is $4,300,000.00. It can be broken down approximately as follows:

Steelwork (incl. dry docking, towing etc.) $600,000.00

Superstructure (incl. insulation, wood, trim etc.). $1,350.000.00

Main Engine and Boilers. $500,000.00

Auxiliary Machinery and Pumps. $400,000.00

Piping and Electrical. $550,000.00

General and Outfitting. $500,000.00

Engineering, Inspection and Insurance. $450,000.00

This estimate does not include the costs of any Sales Taxes, Duties, U.S.C.G. fees, legal fees or cost of re-floating the vessel. Some estimates of costs were obtained from suppliers in present-day dollars. Most of the costs were developed from our knowledge of the scope of work and prevalent charge-out rates and material costs on file and within the marine industry at this time.

ALL ABOARD poster.
Photo by ERNO ROSSI - Cathy Herbert Collection

Crystal Ballroom construction.
Cathy Herbert Collection

Crystal Ballroom in full swing.
Courtesy Buffalo State College, Courier Collection

CRYSTAL BEACH BITS AND BYTES

Narrow Roads At Crystal Beach

The narrow roads at Crystal Beach were first laid out as footpaths and were never intended for automobiles. Most people first arrived there by boat to the Crystal Beach dock or by train to Ridgeway.

Crystal Ballroom

In 1926, the Crystal Ballroom was constructed across the lake from Buffalo, drawing thousands of people from that area. With its dance floor covering 20,000 square feet, crowds of thousands of dancers could be handled with ease.

Buffalo World's Fair Miniature Train

Some things from the purchase of the bankrupt Erie Beach Park ended up at Crystal Beach including a miniature train that was originally used at the 1901 World's Fair in Buffalo. Some games, other rides and the Blue Streak roller coaster known as the Giant, were brought to the park.

Buffalo Evening News July 23rd, 1927

Jelly Roll Morton at Crystal Beach, Ontario.
Dance All Next Week
to the Toe-Tingling, Soul-Stirring Music
by World Famous Jelly Roll Morton and his Red Hot Peppers,
America's Premier Colored Jazz Band.

Dance Marathons

For a number of years the Miss New York State Beauty Pageant was held in the Crystal Ballroom. This pageant drew large crowds as did the dance marathons that were held there as well.

Dance Marathon, 1928

One incident on August 17th of 1928 spoiled the fun for many when the Attorney-General of Ontario ordered a dance marathon to stop in the Crystal Ballroom. There were negative feelings against such things at the time and presumably no more marathons happened in the province after that point. Prize money was distributed equally among the three remaining couples. Despite this, the dance hall still set a new attendance record that year.

Picnics In The 1930's

Picnics were very popular during the 1930's, with the grove capable of seating up to 6000. But it was the beach that drew many more people. It had fine white sand, lifeguards, diving platforms, water slides, and at one point a "Sea Swing" in the water. Next to the beach was a large bathhouse. An advertisement from when it first opened over a decade earlier stated that the bathing pavilion could accommodate 3500 persons. In the 1930s it was enlarged and advertised to accommodate 10,000.

Original Rocket Ships.
Harvey Holzworth Collection

New Rocket Ships.
Harvey Holzworth Collection

Rocket Ships

A new ride was the Chambers Rocket Ship, located between the Magic Carpet and another Chambers attraction, the Laff-in-the-Dark. It consisted of a central 26-meter high tower with six sweeps to which were attached stainless steel cars with a 4 X 2 seating arrangement. They had pointed noses and flaming tails. The tower was enclosed within a pavilion which had a circular walkway one story above the ground where passengers boarded and disembarked. A clock adorned the face of one side of the pavilion.

"Your stomach came up."

Fred Stephens

We rode the Cyclone roller coaster in the 1930's and '40's. Your stomach came up so you could look at it. A very thrilling, very physical bang-you-around ride.

Harold Austin

He served as leader of the Crystal Ballroom house band between 1935 and 1955, playing as well on the Canadiana.

"... trying to get a good tan."

Edythe Oldfield Heuer

My high school sorority used to rent a cottage for 2 weeks in the summer and we also rode the Canadiana over several times. What fun!

I graduated from high school in 1940 so my years at the beach were from 1937 to 1940. Our prime love was trying to get a good tan at the beach.

Once a friend and I rode bikes over to the beach and back to Buffalo. ONCE was enough. I now reside in California but my days at the beach have never left my mind.

Cottage Week

Fraternities and sororities traditionally rented a cottage for at least a week at Crystal Beach.

"Yes, I worked on the most fantastic ride of all."

Frank Thornton

I worked in Hot Dog Alley at Smeaders' Hot Dog stand, owned by Mr. and Mrs. Smeader from Buffalo. I started working there around 1966 in the back of the stand where everything was made on site. This included all the hamburgs, fresh cut French fries and of course Loganberry. My main job was to peel and cut fries. I was only 15 years old at the time and I had arms on me like a truck driver from lifting the 50 lb bags of potatoes. Daily I'd lift, peel and cut 5 to 7 bags weighing 200 to over 300 lbs in total. I'd cut them and place them in 25 gallon lard buckets. Then I covered them with water to prevent them from turning brown. I placed them in the walk-in cooler until they could go up front to be blanched.

At least twice per season we would make Loganberry concentrate, the stuff that you would buy to mix with water to make the drink. Mrs. Smeader's son would show up to give a hand and we would spend the whole day making gallons of the stuff. We'd mix sugar and extract of Loganberry to get it made.

Mrs. Smeader kept the old-fashioned 5-gallon glass tank with a metal cover to contain the Loganberry — with a ladle to scoop it out. The drink was kept cold by putting in blocks of clear ice. We had to taste the mixture as the ice melted to assure that the quality remained high. From time to time we added more concentrate to the tank. It had to taste just right or she would give us a royal reprimand. It was fun drinking the ice cold Loganberry and it was free.

I grew up in Crystal Beach. As a kid, I waited for the warm days of spring to rush down to "The Park" as we called it, to get a great summer job. In my first year inside "The Park," I started at 80 cents an hour. But the bonus was the fun we had after the Park would close at night — at the beach parties and the GIRLS.

I started there on the Merry-G0-Round collecting tickets after the ride started moving. After a few days you were good enough at timing your step to get on and off the ride as it moved at a fast speed. By the end of the first week you could get on and off with two cold drinks in your hand. That's what you call balance.

I worked my way up through the pecking order in the Park and landed a job on the most fantastic ride of all, THE COMET. This was the best place to work as a 15 and 16-year-old guy because the chicks thought that you were way toooo cool if you worked there. This made for some late nights getting home after the place closed.

I rode the Comet every day a countless numbers of times. I would ride in the last car at least 3 times a day to oil the Comet tracks.

The Comet is listed as one of the world's best wooden coasters even to this day. People say that it was made out of steel. The supporting structure is made out of steel but the bed that the track is built on is made of laminated wooden planks and is therefore a wooden coaster.

My main job was to check the cars for lost goods after each ride was finished. All the stuff in the front 2 cars would be on the floor at the front of the car. Yet all of the stuff on the floor in the back 2 cars was on the floor in the back of the car. There were tons of Zippo lighters.

My final job in my last years of high school lasted well into the fall after Labor Day, when the Park was closed for the season. That's when I worked in the Penny Arcade. I was really interested in electronics. When I worked there it was owned by E.G.& J. Knapp Co. of Crystal Beach. They also had arcades in Niagara Falls and every year at the Canadian National Exhibition in Toronto. I worked for one of the owners, Elden Knapp who was a really great guy. I was one of the "mechanics" as we were called. If your coin got stuck or the machine did not work right, I would get you going again.

Then I left the area in 1976.

"Gone but not forgotten"

Jack Ahlers

I began to go to Crystal Beach in the 1940's, when Mom would take Sis and me by Greyhound from Angola to Buffalo, then to the Canadiana dock. I always enjoyed the ride over and back. I was fascinated by the overhead view of the engine mechanism when I looked down at the shaft in the middle of the boat.

When I first began our excursions the Cyclone remained supreme. Ever since then I have preferred wooded coasters to the modern steel structures. More "character." Another thing that I loved in retrospect was the relatively uncrowded nature of the park in comparison to that of modern day mega-theme parks. By the time that I got into high school, the Crystal Beach Boat was used for evening cruises, mostly by guys and their dates. It was nice for a while but as with so many other things the atmosphere began to change towards the impolite, unruly groups. Yeah, it used to be a kinder, gentler world.

The sun sets on Crystal Beach.
Rick Herbert Collection

Five Pin Bowling

Fran Baumler

As kids we saved coupons, pop bottles, newspapers and rags to get enough money to spend a day at Crystal Beach. Then I discovered 5 pin bowling in the town and their need for pin boys. I would take the early boat across from Buffalo and work all day as a pin boy. Then I'd take the last boat home to Buffalo.

Crystal Beach Hipsters

Hipsters in the late 1940s and 1950's wore pegged leg or draped pants with 24 inch knees and 14 inch cuffs, in colors from pink to chartreuse. Belt loops dropped two to three inches from the waist.

Male hipsters wore their hair long, greased back with fenders into a D.A., a duck's anus, that was full at the back of the head and neck, sometimes called a boogie cut. Crew or brush cuts were for squares.

Squares wore khakis with a striped shirts or V-necked sweaters. Many squares were starting to wear jeans or "dungarees" with the cuffs turned up, once those squares lost the fear of being called farmers.

Girls exchanged clothing in friendship, with corduroy sorority jackets trading hands in great numbers. Often friends wore identical clothes and saddle shoes. Thanks to Marlon Brando as leader of a biker gang, the black leather jacket became acceptable for both sexes.

Car buffs can tell the date of this photo.
Cathy Herbert Collection

The Crystal Flyer.
Cathy Herbert Collection

"...forty seconds of pure terror."

ERNO ROSSI

I visited Crystal Beach with my big brother, Keith Rossi and I gawked at this awesome playground enjoyed by Americans, Canadians and tourists from around the world. I touched the warm sand and breathed the clean air. I watched the innocent fun of people splashing in the clear water. I smelled the aroma of waffles, hamburgs, hotdogs and fries. Then I cringed at the shrieks from the Cyclone roller coaster as it roared down its first hill. I looked up at my brother Keith who asked me if I was brave enough to join him on the Cyclone. I screamed, "Yes," over the clackety-clack of the midway noise.

Keith locked me into my seat with a lap-bar and then sat beside me. I twitched with excitement as we climbed the first hill. I grasped the lap-bar and tried to scream as the bottom dropped out of my world to certain death. That plunge dropped into Lake Erie but we were saved by a sharp right turn and forty seconds of pure terror.

Then Keith pried my hands from the lap-bar, lifted me from my seat and carried me down the long ramp to safety. I was too rigid to walk. "Did you like that?" he asked. I shook my head up and down. "Do you want to go again?" I shook my head sideways. I was too terrorized to speak. Keith looked up at the Cyclone as if to say goodbye and said, "The Cyclone is finished this year. They'll take it down and build a new roller coaster." The year was 1946.

Matching Track Suits

One time when I was a kid I was waiting in line for the Giant coaster. There was a total New York State couple in line wearing shiny yellow and black matching track suits. I thought it was pretty awesome. Seemed like lots of American couples wore matching outfits.

"Every kid in Dunkirk was Catholic"
Anonymous, 1968

It always amazed me that every year when the Catholic youth organization (CYC) announced the annual Crystal Beach Day, suddenly every kid in Dunkirk N.Y. was Catholic and on those buses. Go Figure!

But no trip to Crystal Beach aboard the CYC bus was ever complete until the bus had returned through American Customs at the border and they didn't find all the firecrackers and M-80's stuffed in our socks and underwear.

My favorite was the Magic Carpet-Fun House. I'd wait until a good looking older girl wearing a skirt came along and being a gentleman, I'd let her go ahead of me and the jets of air from the floor would blow her skirt sky high—Wow!! Hey I was 12... OK? And I wasn't getting any yet.

There was a bench on the second floor patio overlooking the gardens that was one of my favorite spots to hang out... because no sooner did someone sit down on that bench than a jolt of electricity surged through their buns sending them on your way. The metal screws in the bench were wired with an electrical current.

Ballroom Fire

A fire in 1974 destroyed the dance floor of the Crystal Ballroom. It was repaired and dancing resumed.

Bumper Cars
Mrs. Riley

When I let my kids ride the bumper cars I knew why that was their favorite ride. They came crashing into mom with that wild animal look in their eyes.

Having a go on the Calypso.
Cathy Herbert Collection

"Crystal Beach was a very happy time."

Carol

It's amazing how we clearly remember what happened at Crystal Beach almost sixty years ago. And then we forget why we went to the other room or why we opened the refrigerator. Crystal Beach was a very happy time of my life.

"... during the summer of 1972."

A. Nicks, Tonawanda N.Y.

I worked at Crystal Beach Park during the summer of 1972. It was probably the best time of my life. I was a "mechanic" in the arcade. On rainy Tuesdays, with no guests in the park, I would spend my time playing the baseball game, where the metal ball would pop out and you had to hit it with a bat. Kinda like pinball.

"... inhale your trash."

Rachel, Indianapolis, Indiana

My little brother Eric was about 3 years old and he'd run around Crystal Beach and asked people for their garbage so that he could feed Leo the Lion, the garbage can that would inhale your trash.

"..staring death in the face..."

Tim Russert in, *Big Russ And Me*

Riding the Comet coaster was like staring death in the face and surviving.

"Riding the Wild Mouse."

Tim Russert in, *Big Russ And Me*

You felt like you were hanging over thin air with nothing between you and the ground.

Westinghouse

Brian Pawlowski, Hamburg, N.Y.

My father worked at Westinghouse and we used to come to Crystal Beach every Westinghouse Day.

Lovejoy Days

Mrs. Tagliarino

I used to come to Crystal Beach on the bus on Lovejoy neighborhood days.

"...my first kiss with a Canadian boy!"

Kathy Lovejoy

It was in the Laff in-the-Dark where I had my first kiss with a Canadian boy. The other thing that I will always remember was the air jets that blew up your skirt when you were walking through the Magic Carpet. And all the giggles it caused even hours later. Saving my babysitting money all year was well worth going to Crystal Beach that summer.

"As teenagers we looked forward to Saturday nights..."

Mary Wintle

As teenagers we looked forward to Saturday nights when we could get all fixed up to go dancing and hopefully meet some nice boy. The dance hall was so shiny and up above glittered the huge crystal ball.

Ferris Wheel at night.
Photo by and courtesy of Alfred F. Sagon-King

" *I earned one dollar an hour there in 1969.*"

Lorraine Murphy

I worked for Mr. Parker at the fishpond. He ran the Skeeball too. I earned one dollar an hour there in 1969.

" It was our Disney World"

Patty Bizub

Our family had a cottage there at Crystal Beach. They would give us a couple of bucks and we'd be gone all day. It was safe. It was our Disney World.

"...my Crystal Beach memories kept me sane in Vietnam."

Jay Wopperer

When I was in Vietnam, I missed my parents, my girlfriend and Crystal Beach. My Crystal Beach memories kept me sane in Vietnam.

"I won the Comet Challenge"

Larry Shisler

I won the Comet Challenge in 1986 by riding the Comet roller coaster, 186 times between July, 8, 1986 and August 8, 1986. But July 16, 1986 was my best day when I rode it 122 times.

The round trip on the Comet took about one minute and forty-five seconds. With loading and unloading the round trip took about three to five minutes.

"I worked On The Flying Bobs."

Phil

I worked at Crystal beach Park for the last 6 years that the park was in operation. I still have four of my uniform shirts, two red and two green with my name tag. I worked on The Flying Bobs.

"We yearly fell in love with some boy from Canada."

Nancy Janish

Summer was not summer without going there and riding the rides, roller skating and of course, meeting boys.

I never got to ride the boat as it was taken out of service after they had the riot on it. But my aunt was on the boat the day of the riot and I heard all the stories about how much she was frightened.

However my friends and I did go every year on a bus trip that the Town of Riverside ran. Everyone from Riverside High School went and what fun we did have! You bought a ticket and the bus ran all day long. So you could go over early and come back whenever you wanted to. My girlfriends and I would go very early in the day and roller skate half the day and ride the rides the rest of the day. We yearly fell in love with some boy from Canada who we never saw again. Ha Ha. We had a blast and never missed a year.

I remember the Comet. We would ride it over and over again until it actually became tame. We loved the Magic Carpet which dumped you at the end onto a carpet that you rode like the wind was under it. And of course I have to mention the Laff-in-the-Dark. That was when we got to sneak a kiss with the boyfriend we would never see again. Oh what times we had there. Miss them so much and feel really sorry for the kids today that they will never experience the fun of Crystal Beach.

"... the live pony ride."

Fran Porebski

Each summer during the mid 1950's to mid 1960's I would look forward to my visits to Crystal Beach. I loved the thrill of the rides and those warm powdered sugar waffles.

But tradition required time spent in the arcade playing the pinball machines and rolling up the scores in Ski-ball. Miniature golf with my cousin was also a must. Grandmother always made us go with her on the big Rocket ride by the Magic Carpet.

Visits with my family always included a walk into town to have steak sandwiches at Nate's. Loved to go on the Ferris wheel at night and see the entire park lit up in lights. Then there were the community events held during community days in the area across from the park. I even remember sitting in the back seat of my father's car and smelling of the final ride of many evenings…the live pony ride.

"borders don't have much meaning."

Ed Degenhart

What is wonderful to see is that borders don't really have much meaning. Many of us grew up in Buffalo and in many places in Canada too. My family had a cottage at Long Beach just west of Port Colborne. Childhood memories like this are priceless.

164

Stan Kenton poster.
Photo by ERNO ROSSI - Cathy Herbert Collection

"...playing Rock Around The Clock."

Eileen Gale

The boat ride, playing Rock Around The Clock all the way over to the beach and dancing all the time. We had different cottages during the years and made many friends along the way. The Jersey shore cannot take the place of Crystal Beach for me. Buffalo and Western New York is a great place to live and I'm glad that I grew up there.

"First love."

Irka Davis

First love. In 1969-70-71, I and a group of gals rented a cottage at CB for the entire summer. There were all boy and all girl cottages. We had wonderful parties and went to the park very often indeed. I remember the Wild Mouse. I love that ride! And I remember the roller skating rink where I saw people skating backward. It looked so easy. Well it wasn't. I fell and got a heck of a bruise when I tried it.

Laff-in-the-Dark cars.
Rick Herbert Collection

"... the brush burns on my butt."

Sharon Krawczyk

I remember the first year that the Texas Revolver was there. It must have been around 1977. I was really afraid to go on it for the first time. But once I did, I ended up riding about ten times that day.

I remember the Rotor and hanging on the wall when the floor dropped and the brush burns on my butt from riding it so many times.

The Wild Mouse was a bit too scary for me, although I did ride it a few times. Then there was the sitting version of the Roundup next to the Giant Coaster. And one of my favorite rides was the Monster near the Comet.

I rode the HEYDEY tons of times with my mom. And we both found the Skyride kind of scary.

"Uncle Vinny tried to be one of the kids."

Colleen

The last time that we went up to Crystal Beach was in the late 1980's and my Uncle Vinny decided to be one of the kids. Well, he went down one of the water slides and it was such a rush that at the bottom he opened his mouth real wide and seemed to take in a lot of water. He stood up and kept looking around in the water. We were wondering what he was looking for and he pointed to his mouth. He had lost his false teeth.

After getting over the hysterical laughter we had to wait until the ride closed and his son finally found his teeth. He was so happy that he held them up for all of us to see and everyone applauded. He then put them back into his mouth.

"Bug City."

Carol Winiarski

One thing that really sticks in my mind is when my neighbor from across the street (Tony) took his niece, nephew and myself to Crystal Beach. He bought us a sucker and we were eating it on the Sky Ride at night. Guess what happened when the Sky Ride made the turn to make its way back to the beginning? It was night time and a light was on at the curve. Yes, you've got it. Bug City. I had bugs all over my sucker and that sucker was history.

Skyride and Comet.
Cathy Herbert Collection

"Last ride on the Comet"

Jim McDonnell

Allow me to share a great memory that I have of the park. As luck would have it, my brother and I took the second last ride ever on the Comet at Crystal Beach. We were lucky enough to sit in the front seat. We thought it was the last ride ever, but there was such an uproar from those in attendance that they sent off one more ride.

I found out later from a number of friends that someone had taken a picture of me and my brother sitting in the front seat on that second to the last ride and had submitted the picture at an event at the Erie County Fair in Hamburg N.Y. To this day I have never see that picture but would love to get my hands on a copy. Should fate be on my side the picture would be a family keepsake. If I'm lucky, someone out there has this picture. If they would be so kind and allow me to get a copy. Thanks. I can be emailed at jimmymc@adelphia.net.

The Giant Coaster

The Giant roller coaster, 1916-1989 holds the record of 74 seasons in use.

168

Most Coasters

Of the closed parks, Crystal Beach holds the record of 10 for the most coasters used there from the early 1900's through 1989.

The Cyclone

Of the defunct wooden roller coasters the Cyclone holds the speed record of 84 kmh or 50 miles per hour.

"...not even The Beast or Son of The Beast"

Tony Krzywowiaza

I was old enough to ride the Comet for the first time in the mid 1980's. I remember getting in the short line for the ride and then getting off and going back on for many, many rides in a row. I have since been to many Six Flags Parks across the US and no roller coaster even comes close to the Comet. Not even the Beast or Son Of The Beast at Kings Island in Ohio. The Comet was the first coaster that I rode, in which you could choose to ride forward or backward. I wish I was around when the Cyclone was there.

I really miss Crystal Beach because it was not crowded. Here on the west coast, especially at Disneyland, you have to wait at least 30 to 45 minutes to get on a ride.

"Recording Twist and Shout"

Amy

Seeing pictures of the Comet, I feel the same way that I did during my first ride. I remember recording, "Twist and Shout" in the recording booth in the park.

"...as if it were yesterday."

Cheryl

Crystal Beach brings back warm memories of childhood. The Comet, Skyride and cotton candy are still vivid in my mind. My eighth grade class from LaSalle Junior high School traveled there and I still remember that day as if it were yesterday. Where does all the time go?

"Johnnie Ray"

Myra

I remember "Jacks" and his grilled hot dogs. Remember the mirror on the side of the snack bar? We would comb our wet hair with not a care in the world. I remember Irwin Sandler so well, imitating Johnnie Ray by singing, "Cry." Oh what happy memories.

My husband and I went to Bay Beach last year and watched the kids play on the "rock." I had tears in my eyes thinking about how my mother used to watch me in the water and I could not go past the big rock.

"... the room of mirrors."

Bernie

I remember the Magic Carpet, later renamed the Magic Palace. It contained the room of mirrors that made anyone who stood in front of them look fat, thin or whatever. I also recall the "slanted" room where, because of the way it was built, you had to run down one aisle and struggle to walk up the next isle.

Also, who could forget why it was called the Magic Carpet? At the exit, you sat on this bench made up of steel rollers. The entire bench unfolded into a ramp and you slid down it onto the magic carpet and glided out the exit. What a great ride!

"... order pitchers of Canadian beer."

Carol Pastore

Gosh, I sure remember Crystal Beach and the Canadiana. Most of my teen years were spent dancing on the Canadiana and at the Crystal Beach Ballroom with Maynard Ferguson, a trumpet player who hit those high notes quite often.

Our dates would go to the pub and order pitchers of Canadian beer and play chug-a-lug. Sometimes, we would miss the boat back to Buffalo.

We had a wonderful childhood and it didn't cost much. As we grew older we would drive there to friend's cottages and play poker. My aunt owned a cottage there and my mother would spend a week or so with her.

Poster advertising the Canadiana.

Photo by ERNO ROSSI

The Telephone Union Picnic Poster.

Photo by ERNO ROSSI - Harvey Holzworth Collection

Sun and fun at Crystal Beach, 1975.
Cathy Herbert Collection

The Happy Gang Poster.
Photo by ERNO ROSSI - Cathy Herbert Collection

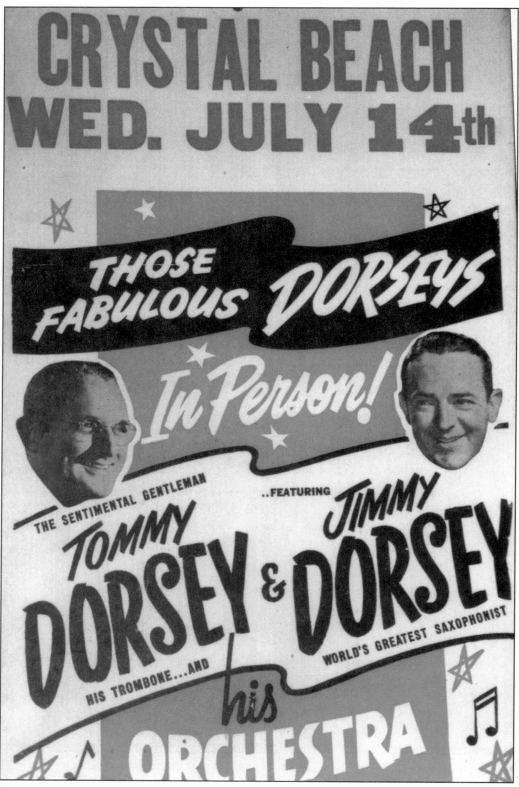

Poster advertising the Dorsey's.

Photo by ERNO ROSSI, Harvey Holzworth Collection

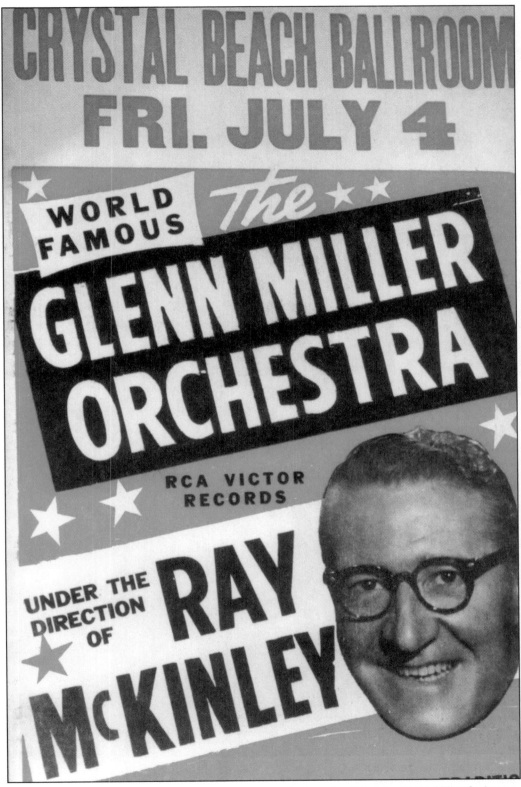

Poster advertising the Glenn Miller Orchestra.
Photo by ERNO ROSSI, Harvey Holzworth Collection

TOP: The Laff in the Dark ride.
BOTTOM: The Magic Palace.

Cathy Herbert Collection

TOP: Paul Bunyan greeted guests at the park.
BOTTOM: Enjoying the famous Sugar Waffles.

Cathy Herbert Collection

The Auction Brochure from the sale of Crystal Beach Park.

1888 • CRYSTAL BEACH PARK • 1989

NEAR NIAGARA FALLS AND BUFFALO, NY

THE COMET COASTER

One of the world's most famous coasters, the Comet is rated by the American Coaster Enthusiasts (ACE) as one of the top ten coasters. Built by the Philidelphia Toboggan Company (PTC) in 1946, the coaster features a steel super structure. The comet stands 107' H with an initial drop of 97', set at an angle of over 50 degrees, speeds on the comet reportedly reach 60 MPH. It is approx. 4800' in length and features several 70' drops. The (3) trains can run forward or backwards. Removal time negotiable.

THE GIANT COASTER

One of the last two remaining side friction coasters in North America, the Giant was built in 1916 of wood. It is approx. 3300' L and the highest drop is approx. 60'. It features (3) trains. Removal time negotiable.

SAW MILL RIVER FLUME

The O.D. Hopkins Saw Mill River opened in 1982 at a cost of $1.5 million. Total length is approx. 1050' with two lifts and 13 "log" cars. All pumps, conveyors, motors, etc., included along with controls and buildings. Removal time negotiable.

SUPER DUPER WATERSLIDE

Build in 1978, this 4-flume waterslide is built on a hillside with wooden stairs to the top. There are three slides averaging 380' L each that snake around each other. A separate children's slide is approx. 88' L. All pumps, motors, filters, etc. Slides are constructed of sectionalized fiberglass. Removal time negotiable.

MAJOR RIDES

- ☐ Huss Pirate Ship, Trailer Mounted (3 Trailers) 1978, s/n 3745, Recently Repainted
- ☐ O.D. Hopkins Sky Ride, 15 Cars, 6 Towers, New Cable 1987, Approx. 1000' L
- ☐ Chance Flying Bobs, Trailer Mounted (2 Trailers), Bought New By Park in 1980, New Top 1989, s/n 80-2757
- ☐ Sartori Adult Chair-O-Plane Swing, 1976
- ☐ Everly Monster, Trailer Mounted Center and 2 Pup Trailers, s/n 10600
- ☐ A.H. Merry-Go-Round, 36 Aluminum Horses + 4 Kiddie Ponies, 3 Row-All Jumpers, Sound System, 1956
- ☐ (20) Soli Bumper Cars
- ☐ Eli Scrambler, s/n 28-56
- ☐ Hollingsworth Cinema 180 Dome Theatre
- ☐ Big Eli No. 5 Ferris Wheel, Wood Seats with Hairguards, s/n 784-47, A Classic in Excellent Condition
- ☐ Sellner Tilt-A-Whirl, Steel Platforms, s/n 90165
- ☐ (8) Ward Mfg. Electric, Rechargable Wet Boats, 1979
- ☐ 1939 Chambers "Laff-In-The-Dark" Dark Ride, 12 Cars, An American Classic with "Laughin' Sal" and Two Other Animated Figures, Tricks, Illusions, Etc.
- ☐ Magic Carpet Walk-Thru, Another Classic Amusement Park Attraction, Tilting Room, Tipping Wall, Air, Slide, Mirror Maze, Bar Maze, Etc., Excellent Neon Signs
- ☐ Gebr-Jhle Bruchsal (Hot Rods Inc.) Antique Electric Cars (6)
- ☐ Hrubetz Tip Top, Trailer Mounted, New Center 1989, s/n 912, 1966

KIDDIE RIDES

- ☐ 1988 Wafabco Moon Walk
- ☐ Wafabco Castle Inflatable Ball Crawl
- ☐ A.H. Skyfighter, s/n 1003550
- ☐ Barbiera Kiddie Karousel, (42) Animal Figures on 32'x32' Aluminum Platform
- ☐ Mack Carousel, (14 Cars) Helicopter, Firetruck, Sports Cars, School Bus, Go Cart, Etc., with Portable Building
- ☐ A.H. Wet Boats, Portable Tank
- ☐ Everly Lady Bug, 1978
- ☐ A.H. Little Dipper Coaster

THE END OF A GREAT ERA

CRYSTAL BEACH PARK

FOOD SERVICE EQUIPMENT

Icee Machines; SS Self Contained Draft Beer Cases; Fryers; Popcorn; Floss; Ice Machines; SS Sinks; SS Prep Tables; Taylor Ice Cream Machines; Pretzel Ovens; Taylor Frozen Custard Machines; Jet Spray Dispensers; Char Grills; Pizza Ovens; Copper Candy Kettles; Nachos Warmers; Exhaust Hoods; Refrigerators; Freezers; Coffee, Ice Tea and Hot Chocolate Machines; Walk-in Coolers and Freezers; Portable Hot Food Boxes; Dishwashers; Warming Lights; Counters; All Types of Related Equipment in Quantities!

PARK MISCELLANEOUS

(400) Wood Picnic Tables; Park Benches; Cash Registers; Signs; Sound and Stage Equipment (2) 30'x80' Yellow and White Tents, Like New Never Outside; (2) Life Size Bavarian Dancer Statues; Life Size Cowboy On Horse; Large Tin Soldier Statues; Leo the Lion and Porky Pig Circus Wagon Paper Eaters; Flags; Street Lights; (25) Baby Strollers; Golf Carts; Turnstiles; Wood Planters; Trash Receptacles; Gift Shops; Picnic Shelters; Office Equipment; Inventories; Etc.

SHOP EQUIPMENT

Metal and Wood Lathes; Table Saw; Heliarc 250 HF; Welding Equipment; Anvil; Drill Press; Band Saw; Air Compressor; Grinders; Chain Falls; Cherry Picker; Benches; Steel Stock; Power Hack Saw; Vises; Chargers; Nuts/Bolts; Parts; Paint; Supplies; Etc.

ANTIQUES & MEMORABILIA

Cast Iron Street Lights; Cast Iron 4-Place Drinking Fountains; Fun House Mirrors; Art Deco Candy Apple Cases; Signs; Building Salvage; Etc.

GAMES

☐ Princeton Machine Co. 28' Tandem Axle Game Trailer with Darts and Baskets

☐ McGlashan 14-Gun Shooting Gallery, Miedeval Theme

☐ Boom Ball, 4-Unit Coin Operated

☐ Bob's Space Racers. 7-Unit Whac-A-Mole

☐ Derby Racer, 15-Unit Coin Operated

☐ Remote Control Tanks, 6-Unit Coin Operated

☐ Other Games

VEHICLES

☐ 1986 Ford Ranger, V-6, Automatic, With Cap

☐ 1964 GMC Model 7000 Tilt Cab Tractor, Gas, 5-Speed Transmission

☐ 1967 GMC Dump Truck

☐ Other Older Utility Trucks

☐ Wagons

ARCADE

Over 120 Modern and Antique (Collectible) Coin-Operated Machines. Including Horoscope; Nervetests; Lovetests; Guns; Card Vendors; Skee Ball Alleys; Photo Machines; Video Games; Electronic Pins; 4'x8' Slate Pool Tables; Baseballs; Punching Bags; Rayovac Bear Guns; Mutoscope; Monkey Lifts; Foot Vibrators; Guess Your Weight Scales; I.D. Stampers; Genco Grandma; Rotary Merchandisers; Grip Test; Love Meters; Bally Topic Pin; Chicago Baseball; Cranes, Etc.

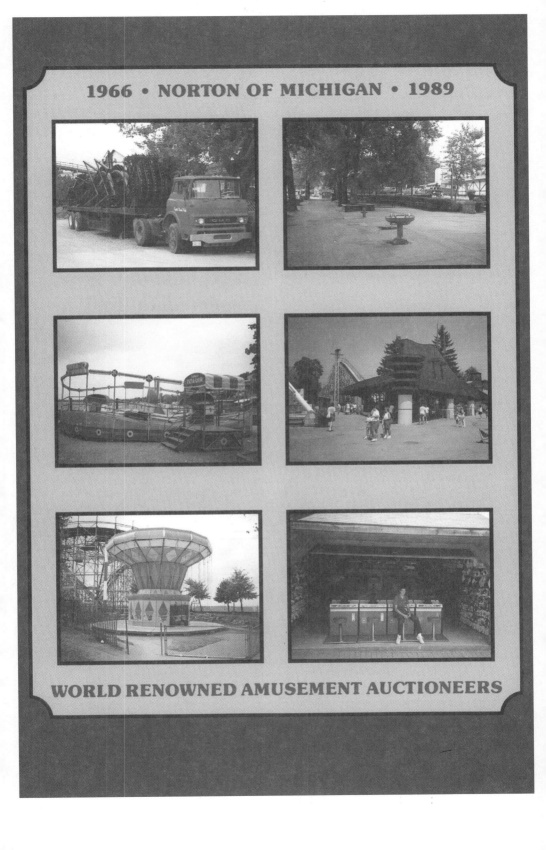

1966 • NORTON OF MICHIGAN • 1989

WORLD RENOWNED AMUSEMENT AUCTIONEERS

Nostalgic Memories

James Saunders

The only thing bad about nostalgic memories is that you have to get older to have them.

"We met two French guys..."

Cyndy Bunch

I moved from Hamburg N.Y. when I was 19 years old. But I still go home every summer. My fondest memory of the beach was with my best friend Debs. We were 12 years old and traveled unchaperoned on a bus to Crystal Beach. What a blast! We met two French guys and we still have memories today. I guess that's what great about Buffalo and Western New York. Bonds. I live in India now with my memories.

The Wild Mouse.
Courtesy Buffalo State College, Courier Collection

"...animals to feed."

Susi (Field) Huntz

The children's' area was so nice for kids and of course the animals to feed. My mom took me on the Wild Mouse when I was about six and she told me that when we went down the first hill, she almost lost me because I was just sitting on her lap with no seatbelts. I can just hear the lawyers over that one.

Nickel Day At The Park

Another nice thing in the good old 1940's was "Goodwill Day" when all the rides were each 5 cents. This occurred on the Wednesday before Labor Day during the final week for the park each summer.

This was the way that the park and its concession ride owners showed their appreciation for a good season. This day was coined, "Nickel Day."

"Buy a photo of yourself taken during the ride."

Dan Fitzmore

Right now we live near The Great Escape theme park near Lake George, N.Y. which is the present home of the Comet. We are happy to say that we have introduced the thrill of the Comet to our daughters, who both consider it their favorite ride at The Great Escape. I can say that the coaster is in fine condition and enjoys great popularity. Its history at Crystal Beach and the old Cyclone are proudly displayed.

The only changes from Crystal Beach are that they use 2 sets of cars, plus they speeded up the ride up the first hill. But there's no Lake Erie to look out over. Also the cars are new with modern restraints and a mid seat divider, so you can't slam your body weight into someone who sat beside you if you sat on the left side. Darn!

Fortunately, no shoulder restraints are used so that you can feel the air as you crest over the hills. You can also buy a photo of yourself taken during a ride.

Kiddieland Motorbikes, 1971.
Rick Herbert Collection

Kiddieland Boats, 1969.
Rick Herbert Collection

Halls Sucker Stand.
Rick Herbert Collection

"The Sucker Wars"

Rick Doan - Crystal Beach Booster

My parents took me to Crystal Beach when I was a child. As a teenager I'd go there with a few girl friends and experiment with alcohol to put it politely. With marriage and children I'd take them to Crystal Beach. When the other large amusement parks started up, I'd take my kids to these big parks, but my kids preferred the great old rides of Crystal Beach.

In 1989, when Crystal Beach was closed up, I felt bad about it and came to the auction with $200 US in my pocket. Basically, everything was beyond my price because of the nostalgia. People were paying crazy prices for stuff. After the auction however, I was able to purchase a Laff-in-the-Dark car from the guy who bought the whole ride. I also bought a Giant roller-coaster car that I store in my garage. Then I got serious about collecting and in the past 15 years I have amassed quite a few things.

I was chairman of Crystal Beach Memory Days for two years. We displayed everything that we had saved from the Park. In 2000 a partner and

I made a video called One Last Ride. Each year we try to put on a different display. This year Cathy Herbert (Miss Crystal Beach) and I went out and bought what was left of The Magic Palace, built in 1947. It remained until 1989 when the Park closed. It was a walk through attraction, with unique rooftop pieces with an Arabian theme. Originally called The Magic Carpet it was renamed the Magic Palace in the 1970's because the carpet was removed after many injury claims were launched against Crystal Beach. People were starting to sue for anything. At auction, it went for $7500 US dollars to John Ramsey of Rochester N.Y. He has since sold it to Cathy Herbert and me for $5000 US. We returned with four of the mirrors and some of the unique roof top pieces and some of the stunts that were on the inside. We have restored some of the roof top art and each year we will restore another piece.

From an 8 track tape, Paul Kassay and I produced a Laughing Sal CD. On Halloween night, I drove up and down the streets of Crystal Beach and amplified the laughter of Laughing Sal. The CD and Video are both available from www.crystalbeachpark.net.

Bob Steckley had talked to the Fort Erie Museum about making Crystal Beach suckers and selling them through the museum. In the meantime, Annie's Antiques in Crystal Beach had a sucker mould, probably not the original mould. Annie's donated it to the museum and it started to make suckers. Boy did those suckers sell!

In the first year the museum made fifteen thousand dollars on suckers. They bought another building and called it, "The Museum That Suckers Built."

In the meantime, Bob Steckley was working with the Hall's family to get the moulds for the original suckers. When he got the moulds and the original recipe he talked to the museum about retailing his suckers. The museum declined the offer and continued to sell their own suckers called Crystal Beach Suckers, a name that they trade marked. Bob called his suckers, Hall's Suckers, the original name with the original recipe. Soon sucker sales for the museum went tits up. The museum immediately lost interest in anything to do with Crystal Beach and even refused to display donated artifacts about Crystal Beach. I point this out occasionally in a column that I write. I say that the museum is no longer interested in The Crystal Beach Park. Such was the effect of The Sucker Wars.

Advertisement for Les Brown and his Band of Renown - Just one of the many groups that played the Crystal Ballroom over the years.
Photo by ERNO ROSSI

Crystal Beach Sign displayed the sale of Suckers, Waffles & Taffy.
Photo by ERNO ROSSI

WILD MOUSE foreground, COMET to the left and boat-dock in background.
Cathy Herbert Collection

The entrance to the
Crystal Beach Park.
Cathy Herbert Collection

Poster of Frank Wojnarowski.
Photo by ERNO ROSSI -
Cathy Herbert Collection

Johnnie Ray poster.
Photo by ERNO ROSSI - Cathy Herbert Collection

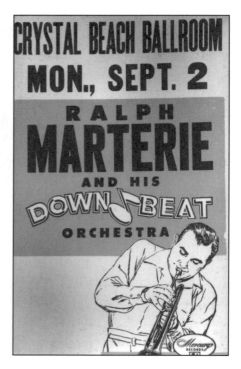

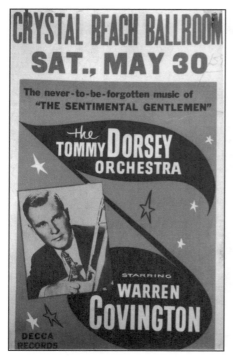

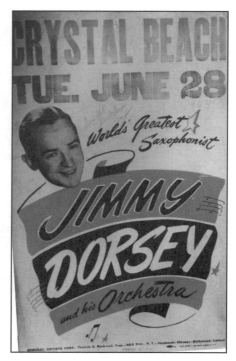

Photos by ERNO ROSSI - Cathy Herbert Collection

My Crystal Beach Memories

My Crystal Beach Memories